Making Time to Lead

This book is dedicated to future principals
who make the time to lead.

Making Time to Lead

How Principals Can Stay on Top of It All

Richard A. Simon   James F. Newman

CORWIN PRESS
A Sage Publications Company
Thousand Oaks, California

For information:

Corwin Press
A Sage Publications Company
2455 Teller Road
Thousand Oaks, California 91320
www.corwinpress.com

Sage Publications Ltd.
6 Bonhill Street
London EC2A 4PU
United Kingdom

Sage Publications India Pvt. Ltd.
B-42, Panchsheel Enclave
Post Box 4109
New Delhi 110 017 India

Printed in the United States of America

Library of Congress Cataloging-in-Publication Data

Simon, Richard, 1951-
Making time to lead: How principals can stay on top of it
all/Richard A. Simon, James F. Newman.
 p. cm.
ISBN 0–7619–3864–8 (Cloth)—ISBN 0–7619–3865–6 (Paper)
 1. School principals—United States—Handbooks, manuals, etc. 2. School management and organization—United States—Handbooks, manuals, etc. 3. Educational leadership-United States-Handbooks, manuals, etc. I. Newman, James F. II. Title.
LB2831.92.S54 2004
371.2′012—dc21

2003011596

03   04   05   06   10 9   8   7   6   5   4   3   2   1

Acquisitions Editor:	Robert D. Clouse
Editorial Assistant:	Jingle Vea
Production Editor:	Melanie Birdsall
Copy Editor:	Cheryl Duksta
Typesetter:	C&M Digitals (P) Ltd.
Proofreader:	Tricia Toney
Cover Designer:	Tracy E. Miller
Production Artist:	Lisa Miller

Contents

Acknowledgments   ix

About the Authors   xi

Introduction   xiii

1. Organizing   1
   Setting Up Your Organizational System   1
   Make To-Do Lists   3
   Keep Up With Mail   4
   Make Special Folders   4
   Clip, Post, and Save Those Articles   5
   Create Your Own Filing System   6
   Carry Your Desk With You   7
   Technology Can Set You Free   8
   Copying Is the Sincerest Form of Flattery   9
   Be Your School's Historian   10
   Be Ready for Prospective Parents   11
   Note Cards: The Best Invention Since Sliced Bread   12
   The Master Key Is a Must   13
   Student Planners   14

2. Time   17
   Building Your Calendar   17
   Being in Two Places at Once   19
   Meetings   20
   Getting Started   21
   Coffee Shop Time   22
   Telephone Time   22
   Save Your Calendars   23
   Accreditation   24

3. Communication   27
   How to Use a Telephone   27
   Visibility: Leading by Walking Around   28

The Working Lunch 29

Parents as Partners 30

Public Presentations 31

4. Delegation **33**

Questions to Ask 33

Use Your Staff 34

Faculty Meetings Can Be Fun 37

5. Summer **39**

Staff Selection 39

Save Those Resumes 40

Student Placement Records 41

Student Placement Procedures 41

Keeping Your Files Active 42

Getting Ready for the Year 43

Remember Your Own Professional Development 44

6. People **45**

Know Your Faculty and Staff 45

Learn Those Student Names 46

Break Bread Together 47

The Little Things Do Matter 48

Buy Stock in Hallmark 48

Everyone Values a Break 49

Let Them Eat Ice Cream 50

7. Self **51**

Keep a Journal 51

Conferences 52

Study Groups 54

Portfolios 55

Preparing Future Principals 55

Administrative Retreats 56

Pamper Yourself 57

Teach a Class 58

Reading and Sharing 59

Resource A: Today's Agenda **61**

Resource B: Yearly Task List **63**

Resource C: Faculty Note Cards **69**

Resource D: Student Planner Memo   **71**

Resource E: Aspiring Administrator Training Brochure   **73**

Resource F: Administrative Retreat Memo   **75**

Acknowledgments

Corwin Press gratefully acknowledges the contributions of the following reviewers:

Richard Doss
Principal
Brownsburg Jr. High School
Brownsburg, IN

Kevin Peterson
Principal
Red Bank Elementary School
Clovis, CA

N. James Bulger
Principal
Central Middle School
Greenwich, CT

Creig Nicks
Principal
Chapparal Middle School
Moorpark, CA

About the Authors

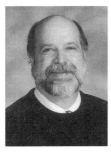 **Richard A. Simon** has been a high school principal for the past twenty years in three states. He is currently the principal of The Wheatley School, an eighth- through twelfth-grade public high school in Nassau County, Long Island. He has also served as principal at Allentown High School in Allentown, New Jersey; at Amity Regional High School in Woodbridge, Connecticut; and at Cherry Hill High School West in Cherry Hill, New Jersey. Mr. Simon holds a master's degree in education from Harvard University. He has received a Geraldine R. Dodge Foundation Fellow for School Leadership Award and a National CBE Fellow for Independent Study in the Humanities grant. Mr. Simon serves as a chair for the new Accreditation for Growth Middle States process and is the coauthor of *The High School Principal's Calendar* (Corwin Press, 2000).

 **James F. Newman** has been an educator for more than twenty-five years, working both as a teacher and a principal. He has been the principal of North Side Elementary School in East Williston, New York, for the last fourteen years. Prior to his current position, he was the principal of Centre Avenue School in East Rockaway, New York, for two years and an elementary teacher in a number of districts on Long Island for twelve years.

Dr. Newman holds a doctorate from Columbia University in the education of the gifted, and he holds two masters' degrees from Hofstra University, one in elementary education and one in educational administration. The title of Dr. Newman's doctoral thesis was "The Metacognitive Abilities of Gifted Educational Leaders."

Dr. Newman has been an invited speaker at a number of national conventions and presented "The Top Ten Ways to Land the Administrative Job of Your Choice" at the AASA convention in New Orleans in February 2003.

Dr. Newman is a longtime resident of New York, currently residing in Long Beach, Long Island.

Introduction

The principal's job has become more complicated and demanding over the past decade. The standards and accountability movement, school security and violence, and an increase in litigation are but a few examples of the issues that make the role of school principal an incredibly demanding one. In short, principals are asked to do more. This book is designed to maximize principals' effectiveness by helping them be well organized, learn what they should and should not delegate, and learn how to take care of their staff and themselves. This book contains practical tips on how to create and find the time to lead—as well as manage—schools.

Effective leadership requires a principal to work toward a coherent vision and direction for the school—and make sure their teachers work toward the same goals. This is time-consuming. The strategies and tips in this book enable principals to carve out the time to function as true leaders and at the same time accomplish the managerial demands of the role.

Getting and staying organized is essential if principals expect to find time to lead. The first chapter gives principals a menu of strategies from which they can create an organization system that helps them in addressing the day-to-day demands. By streamlining the work that principals face, time is freed up to build and nurture a school culture that focuses on instructional leadership. Whether it's using to-do lists to track and monitor the demands of the job or whether it's creating personalized filing systems, all principals—even the most experienced—will find useful, time-saving ideas in this chapter.

Controlling one's calendar is an almost impossible task for a leader. Every group, event coordinator, and committee wants the principal as a member or participant. Chapter 2 explores ways to structure one's daily, weekly, monthly, and yearly calendar to accomplish everything yet produce time for intellectually engaging leadership activities.

Chapter 3 provides advice and suggestions to enhance communication without adding time to an already overcrowded principal's calendar. From creating regular newsletters to sustaining a very visible presence during the school day, the tips in this chapter will keep all-important stakeholders in the loop and enable a principal to focus on the big-picture issues.

Delegation is the key to saving and creating time. Chapter 4 looks at the resources a principal can draw on that often go untapped. Empowering staff not only makes them a stronger part of the school culture, but it also provides a quick and easy way to get many routine tasks done.

Chapter 5 describes ways to use time in the summer to prepare for the school year. Principals can organize many activates, projects, and schedules during the summer—and in turn free up time during the school year to engage in genuine leadership activities.

Taking care of people is often the most demanding task for a principal. Staff, students, and parents want to be known, heard, and validated. Investing time in getting to know one's constituents and doing the little things to acknowledge how important they are lay the groundwork for collectively working on the real challenges facing a school. Chapter 6 provides principals with a number of valuable techniques and practices to build relationships with all parties.

The demands on a principal seem to grow every year. Leading in a time of political and social pressure on schools to achieve more with less in the way of resources and freedom generates incredible stress on a principal. Too many principals put their own professional and personal needs last on their list of demands. Taking care of self is the theme of Chapter 7. This chapter looks at ways a principal can stay energized, refreshed, and engaged. A leader's attitude and mood are powerful forces that set the tone for the leader's work and the school environment.

The conclusion to this book argues that in spite of all the pressure and demands on a principal, there is hope for all who take on this challenge. To be an effective leader, to make the job of a school principal manageable and satisfying, requires thoughtful and creative organizational strategies. These strategies unlock time for true leadership work. Principals, to be effective, must take the time to reflect, to experiment, and to engage all constituents in the process of school growth. Time is the key, and using the strategies in this book will help you create it. Good luck.

Chapter One

Organizing

Managing the day-to-day operation of a school is challenging, even on the best days. The principal has to juggle literally hundreds of issues, problems, and requests, from the mundane to the life threatening. By the end of a school day, a principal has fielded numerous phone calls and visits from staff, students, and parents and has made the many regular committee meetings, class visits, and activities that constitute school life.

Being organized is a must. Whether your school is a small elementary school or a large high school, to be an effective principal you must be proactive in planning and organizing your time. There are far too many expectations and demands of principals for principals to rely on their memory or to take things as they come. In this chapter, we share some time-tested methods that will help you keep the never-ending paperwork requirements under control and allow you to allocate time to attend to the most important activities of an effective leader.

SETTING UP YOUR ORGANIZATIONAL SYSTEM

Creating an organizational system to manage and prioritize day-to-day work is essential if a principal wants to create time to be a leader as well as a manager. Begin with a master calendar that is easy to maintain and portable enough to have with you at all times. This can be as simple as a small, paper academic-year calendar that fits in a pocket to the new, handheld technologies that have the power to store extensive data. The calendar is more than a list of meetings, conferences, and activities. It is also the place to record reminders of time-sensitive tasks and emergency phone numbers as well as the place to jot notes down as the need develops. While a number of companies offer comprehensive systems to stay organized, developing one's own system is just as effective and costs much less.

A to-do list is the next critical organizational tool every principal needs. Whether this consists of a large chart on the wall or a handmade list on a sheet of paper, to-do lists not only help ensure all tasks are identified but also offer a chance to prioritize and sequence work efficiently. To-do lists can help track productivity and form the basis of a yearlong list sequenced by date.

Filing and keeping track of the thousands of pages of paper, reports, and letters that flow to and from the principal's office is another key to an efficient organizational system. All too often, a principal loses valuable time looking for that suddenly vital document or note. Creating an effective filing system, a task often performed in conjunction with a secretary, is very important. Filing methods are personal, but we offer the following suggestions:

1. Have your secretary make a copy of each memo and file it by date in a three-ring binder.

2. Keep folders of current projects close at hand, either on a desktop holder or in your desk.

3. Have your secretary file personnel files that contain evaluations and observations in a locked file cabinet. Keep folders of current employees in one section and retired, resigned, or released staff folders in another section.

Part of creating an organizational system includes how one uses time at work. Scheduling conferences so that there is an ending time, grouping phone calls at an otherwise quiet time, and scheduling time to tour the building each day are just a few of the techniques that help create the time needed to fulfill the leadership role.

- Keep a master calendar that works for you.
- Use to-do lists and save them to create a yearlong list of tasks.
- Design a filing system that works for you and your secretary.
- Be efficient in structuring your work time.

All too frequently, principals find themselves tied up in long meetings that require little input or attention from the principal. Making sure to have work projects with you can offer the principal a chance to complete a quick memo or write notes to staff, parents, or students. The section "Carry Your Own Desk" offers tips on how to make this part of your organizational system.

MAKE TO-DO LISTS

All too often a principal's to-do list ends up in the circular file at the end of the day or week. Make effective use of your lists by systematically organizing and saving them. This helps you develop a yearly planning guide and ensures that annual activities are not forgotten.

Your to-do lists can be formatted in a way that organizes and prioritizes daily, weekly, and long-term tasks. Specifically, create a section for immediate tasks, a section for long-term tasks, and a section for list phone calls you need to make. (See Resource A for a sample.)

Updating your list once or twice a week offers you the opportunity to plan your time and efforts effectively. Because they include important notes and phone numbers, used to-do lists should be filed or placed in a notebook.

The summer is a great time to review your year's worth of to-do lists and plan for the coming year. It's also a chance to create a master yearlong to-do list, which is a great organizational tool that reflects the unique characteristics and culture of your school.

By saving your entire file of daily and weekly lists, you will create your year-long list. One way to make the saving process simpler is to use a loose-leaf notebook to keep all the lists in date order. Then, over the summer, go back through the lists, color-coding key tasks by category. The notebook serves as a record of phone numbers, names, addresses, and other information that might otherwise be hard to find. Combining the lists either by month or topic provides you with a reminder list for the major tasks for the coming year. (See Resource B for an example.)

Your saved to-do lists provide a record of how you allocate and use time. Over time, the lists may become part of the evidence needed to support staffing and budget needs. A master yearlong list can also be divided into monthly tickler files to ensure projects and time-sensitive tasks get started in a timely manner. One principal has his secretary file correspondence in a month-by-month filing system. During the summer, he reviews the files, and, during the following year, he uses them as a tickler file at the beginning of each month.

Many school systems require principals to create yearly objectives. Previous years' collections of to-do lists serve as a great source of ideas to generate these objectives. Take time in the summer to carefully review and organize your to-do lists. Once you have a tentative list of possible objectives, be sure to share the list with your staff and ask for additions and priorities.

- Organize and save your to-do lists.
- Format to-do lists to identify priorities.
- Keep your to-do lists updated.
- Create a master yearlong to-do list over the summer.

Your objectives should reflect not just your own ideas but also those of the entire school staff.

KEEP UP WITH MAIL

The principal often receives an enormous amount of mail. Opening and sorting it—let alone reading it—can be an overwhelming task.

Work closely with your secretary to develop a mail system. Your secretary can save you hours by opening, sorting, and prioritizing the mail. You can then make an initial review of your mail, directing items to appropriate staff. The remaining items can then receive your full attention.

Answering mail is also time-consuming. The more you can dispense with it at the time you review it, the better. Keep typical responses on file in your computer system, so you can create a quick personalization of the letter and keep the pile of return correspondence from getting too high.

E-mail has become both a blessing and a burden. Principals in many areas have joined together to form electronic mailing lists, which make sharing questions, ideas, and information much easier. On the other hand, e-mail creates the opportunity for distractions and lots of spam. Some districts and buildings have internal e-mail only, a great time saver and a way to avoid spam. Taking the time to learn the uses and potential abuses of e-mail will make for efficient use of this potentially valuable tool.

Use your mail as an opportunity to send positive feedback to your staff. Copying the superintendent on complimentary letters sent to staff members is a great way to recognize staff. Sending a copy of a workshop or conference opportunity to staff members tells them you are interested in supporting their professional development.

The occasional letter of complaint should take priority. Before responding, do your homework by investigating the concern. Sometimes a personal call to the writer can resolve the problem. Be sure to alert your supervisor of any action you take because the writer may have sent copies to the board of education and the superintendent.

- Create a system to sort and prioritize your mail.
- Use your mail to support and compliment staff.
- Make the resolutions to letters of complaint a priority.

MAKE SPECIAL FOLDERS

Keeping track of the hundreds of student and staff issues that come your way each week is a challenge. The pile of phone messages and notes that accumulate often measures a principal's day. Too often these messages and notes end up in the trashcan as each is addressed. It doesn't take long, however, for one of the issues a principal has already addressed to suddenly reemerge. How many times do principals wish they had saved the original message?

Keeping all phone messages and notes is a very good idea. Create folders labeled "Special Staff" and "Special Students" to retain all of these messages. Dating the folders and keeping them available gives a principal the original record of phone calls, messages, and meeting notes that may be needed to substantiate information in case of legal action or formal proceedings with a staff member.

As a situation grows into a full-blown crisis, establish a separate folder and keep all notes and phone call messages. Retain this folder well after the crisis has resolved because it is not uncommon for a lawsuit or complaint to rear its head again years later. In cases of student issues, what parents may accept as a resolution while their child is still student may change dramatically once the family is finished with the district.

- Retain your phone messages.
- Organize messages by date and category.
- Anticipate the worst and keep your supervisor aware of the situation.

CLIP, POST, AND SAVE THOSE ARTICLES

A few minutes a week to clip newspaper, magazine, and journal articles provides a principal with the opportunity to provide motivation, inspiration, and commendations. This is also a task that is relatively easy to assign to a secretary or an intern. Be sure the office has subscriptions to all the local newspapers and national magazines and journals. Articles that feature current students, staff, and the school should be clipped, posted, and then filed to create an historical archive. Mailing a copy of the article to the staff member or family of a student featured is an excellent way to create good will.

Designating a bulletin board or space in the office near the teacher mailboxes as a notice board is a great way to share news. Often staff members will respond by posting their own material. This also becomes a place to let people know of staff members or students who are suffering an illness or tragedy or who have good news in their families.

As you read the many journals that are available, stay alert to articles that are relevant to your staff. Sharing the articles with staff members is one way to acknowledge the work they are doing. Have your secretary make copies of the article and send them with a short personal note. As the instructional leader of the school, you are sending the message that serious educational ideas and programs are important. You will find a number of these articles will generate ideas for new programs that benefit your students.

Finding the time to maintain this process can be very simple. Keep a folder with articles in your briefcase and be sure to take it with you when you have tasks that may keep you waiting. For example, a visit to a doctor's or a dentist's office often leaves one with time to kill. You can make a major dent in the folder while you wait and feel that your time was not wasted. Even sitting on line for a car wash provides time to read through a few articles and send them on their way.

Keeping a file of articles that mention the school, from important sporting events to test results, provides you with an important source of material for projects that occur infrequently or demand information that is hard to find. Accreditation activities, school anniversaries, celebrations, and class reunions are just a few of the activities that such a file can assist with.

- Subscribe to all local papers.
- Share good news with all.
- Send staff interesting articles.

CREATE YOUR OWN FILING SYSTEM

The life of a principal involves literally thousands of pages of paper a year. Organizing, filing, and sometimes retrieving paper can be a very frustrating— even an embarrassing—experience. Too often you cannot find that suddenly important paper. What principals need is a method of locating papers so quickly that even their harshest critics will be impressed.

So where to begin? Devise a system that fits your working patterns and stick with it. Keep files of active topics, issues, and projects close at hand. A stand-up file divider on your desk or a file drawer in your desk can accomplish this.

Keep a large to-file box handy, which you can use to drop items in that do not need immediate attention. Periodically, sort through the box, discard items that you know will not be needed, pull those of importance, and have your secretary file the rest. Some principals accumulate paper until the summer and spend a few hours doing their own filing.

Doing your own filing offers you a chance to cull material on a regular basis, which makes it easier to find items. This process also is a great way to refresh your memory and to organize tasks and projects for the coming year. Most magazines and catalogs can be discarded after a year because the magazine articles are often available on the Internet or through various library services and catalogs are updated by companies once or twice a year. Be sure to save all correspondence and memos related to accidents, serious discipline matters, and staff evaluation. It is not unusual for a graduate to sue a district over an accident or injury or for a former staff member to request a reference.

Major projects may require their own filing drawer or system. Keep a couple of portable file boxes handy to use with these projects. This enables you to take your files to meetings and have all key materials readily available. Accreditation activities, construction projects, and major committees are just a few examples of projects that might need their own portable file.

Some principals find a series of three-ring binders efficient for their filing system. Clearly labeling each not only makes filing much easier but also creates an impressive bookcase.

What you elect to file is also an important personal decision. One principal keeps a folder for each class on her desk with pictures of each student. The principal periodically reviews the folders, keeps notes of special accomplishments of the students, and checks off each student she has gotten to know. Another principal keeps copies of every special program and sports activity both as a reminder to write appropriate thank-you and commendation notes and as an historical archive for the school.

> - Do your own filing.
> - Devise a filing system that matches your style and needs.
> - Use care when deciding what to file and what to discard, since this is a powerful decision.
> - Keep pictures of students and staff on file.

CARRY YOUR DESK WITH YOU

Principals rarely spend much time in their offices. A typical day includes a variety of formal meetings and informal contacts with staff, students, and parents. Many times a principal crosses paths with a key player on a particular issue only to find that necessary documents or notes are sitting in a file back in their office.

Create a portable desk for you to make sure that the materials needed to address and resolve issues are close at hand. A slim, three-ring binder with pocket pages and a few sheet protectors will do the trick. Keep those lists of important phone numbers, staff evaluation schedules, the year's calendar, and so on in the sheet protectors. Label each pocket page with current issues and put the appropriate memos or notes in the pocket. Carry the binder to meetings or with you as you visit different areas of the building. You will be able to continue working on pending issues during lulls in meetings and have documents at your fingertips if needed. Your portable desk also makes it simple to take the most important work home and to have a ready resource when that emergency phone call comes during the weekend.

While many formal planning systems are commercially available, creating your own gives you the flexibility to make the system work for you rather than the other way around. Make sure that your binder reflects your school colors and has enough room to add material on a regular basis. Pocket labels include items for immediate attention. There should be a pocket containing material related to the superintendent, the students, the staff, the building administrative team, the next newsletter, and any long-term projects you are working on.

Each page protector provides room for such basic lists as a staff roster, the emergency school-closing phone list, administrative assignments, the school telephone directory, the grading system, a schedule for staff evaluations, the executive board of the PTA, and a list of homeroom assignments.

By having all of the key lists available as well as memos and notes related to the pressing tasks, a principal can make effective use of time that is often wasted. Whether it is sitting in the doctor's office, listening to another repetitive presentation, or waiting to pick up your own child from a music lesson, having your desk with you at all times frees up time to invest in the leadership demands of the job.

- Take your office with you.
- Personalize your portable office.
- Use waiting or downtime to continue your office work.

TECHNOLOGY CAN SET YOU FREE

With a small investment of time and money a principal can take on the role of public relations agent for his or her school. A digital camera, color printer, and an office computer give a principal the tools to produce press releases for local newspapers. In addition, readily available image software programs enable a principal to produce personalized cards for staff and students or create bulletin board displays that feature students and staff.

Begin by purchasing a digital camera, learn to use it, and keep it handy in the office. Create a standard press release form and envelopes addressed to local newspapers. Call the students and staff who are being recognized to your office and not only take their picture but also compose a short caption for the picture using your image software. In a minute or two, the picture can be printed and mailed out with the press release. Most photo-quality printers can print as many as eight photos on one letter-size sheet of photo paper.

One principal annually attends one of his school's musical rehearsals. He takes a series of pictures, and, when students arrive the next morning, a bulletin board display of the show is complete and placed prominently at the front of the school. Another principal sends home both random and formal photographs to parents to acknowledge special events or just to say how well things are going.

Having a digital camera also helps to address vandalism or other incidents that may involve disciplinary or police action. Keeping a file with pictures of graffiti or other damage to equipment and the building may assist a principal in bringing those responsible to justice.

Periodically schools undergo expansion or renovation. Creating an ongoing photographic record of the construction and changes not only functions as great bulletin board material but also provides a record that may help resolve any construction issues or problems.

> - Make public relations a priority.
> - A digital camera has many uses beyond public relations.
> - Be your school's historian.

COPYING IS THE SINCEREST FORM OF FLATTERY

Principals often operate from the belief that every newsletter, speech, memo, or letter has to have new and original content. In most cases, following such an approach is time-consuming and not at all necessary. There are many situations, in fact, where using parts or all of a previous newsletter, speech, or memo is the practical and effective way to go. Add to this the many commercially available sources for letters, newsletters, and speeches, and effective principals can substantially reduce the time needed for these tasks.

Copying is the sincerest form of flattery; just be sure and give appropriate credit to the source. Copying can be in the form of reusing a memo, especially those that serve as annual reports of data, events, results, and so on. Just update the information, and the task is completed. This approach also helps develop an historical record that can be maintained from year to year.

Journal articles provide a rich source of material to use in speeches and reports. Create folders for articles that contain potentially useful information, quotes, and stories. Tear out or copy the article and file it for use at a later time. An example of this is one principal, who speaks each year at the Foreign Language Honor Society's induction ceremony. The principal keeps a folder with articles about foreign languages and is quickly able to find fresh quotes and ideas for the introductory remarks called for at the ceremony.

Conventions and workshops also provide a wealth of material and ideas for use in speeches and memos. Tapes and transcripts of presentations, as well as written materials, are often available. Saving material and organizing it by topic help to create a wealth of research that can be quickly retrieved. An added benefit of conventions is collecting the many give-away items vendors offer. One principal brings a "present" back for each of her administrative staff. Another principal restocks the office supply closet with the giveaways.

Technology also creates an efficient means of securing data and information needed for reports and memos. Many counties or administrative associations have created electronic bulletin board systems. A principal can post a question and within a day or so have data from many area schools on almost any issue. This was a particularly effective tool in helping princi-pals decide on the best approach for handling the anniversary of the September 11, 2001, terrorist attacks. Even though the disaster fell at the start of school, the bul-leting board exchanges between principals provided ideas and strategies to manage the day in an appropriate way.

- Copy material—and give credit—to save time.
- Save journal articles to refer to for speeches and presentations.
- Take full advantage of conventions.
- Use technology to get help from your colleagues.

BE YOUR SCHOOL'S HISTORIAN

Imagine for a moment that your school's fiftieth anniversary is upon you and your board of education and your superintendent expect a dignified and infor-mative celebration. You suddenly realize how much time researching your school's past is going to take. Just finding the names of all the previous princi-pals may be a difficult task.

A little time devoted on a regular basis will make events like this easy to han-dle. Begin by keeping folders for articles, pictures, programs of special events, and so on. Your local newspapers and community association newsletters are a great source of material. Keep a box in your office and save copies of every school pro-gram for concerts, plays, ceremonies, and sports events, filed by year. This system makes for an instant source of information for any special anniversary or event.

Make sure your school has a secured collection of yearbooks. These should be guarded carefully because many times there are few yearbooks left or they disappear or get lost. You will want to have a yearbook on hand if one of your school's graduates emerges as a celebrity.

Many schools have alumni associations. These groups can be wonderful sources of material and help to a principal researching the history of a school. Be sure to create ongoing links with the alumni association and request copies of their newsletters. Class reunions also are a great source of history and mate-rial. Offering to host an event at the school helps forge positive links with out-side organizations.

While most showcases and bulletins boards in a school reflect the current accomplishments and topics in the school, devoting one to the history of the school gives a principal the incentive to save appropriate material and provides visitors with a sense of the school community. Posting articles about successful alumni, teams, schoolwide events, and so on serves as a reminder to students and staff of the collective history of their school.

Maintaining a sign-in book for all visitors to the school is more than just a required security measure. The sign-in book can also serve as a source of information that can assist a principal in contacting alumni.

Saving copies of blueprints for the school is a must. All too often principals engaged in a much-needed building project are unable to locate the drawings for the existing facility. Keep a set of drawings in a secure location and be careful about lending them to others. Whether it is a minor change to create new space or a full-blown construction project, the architects and tradesmen will need the plans to avoid mistakes and problems.

- Save your school's programs and articles about students and staff.
- Tap into your alumni connections.
- Keep your building's blueprints on file.

BE READY FOR PROSPECTIVE PARENTS

Often a school is the most important aspect of a potential homebuyer's decision to purchase. Parents and realtors study test results and school and district rankings when making real estate decisions. As principal, you are expected to be a good salesperson for your school.

Because prospective parents may call or visit your school at any time during the year, keep a supply of informational materials readily available to share with parents. If you are busy, your secretary can give out the material and often eliminate the need for you to talk directly with the parents. The material should include a copy of the district and school calendar; copies of recent newsletters and student publications, such as the student newspaper or literary magazine; and a copy of the school profile used in college applications. These profiles include college entrance examinations, advanced placement course data, and other test data as well as demographic information. Elementary and middle schools should prepare the equivalent of a profile. Many states require schools to develop or provide school report cards. Copies of report cards should be available. Recent newspaper and magazine articles that include mention of your school or district also make for good handouts.

Time permitting, the principal should personally meet prospective parents because more often than not they end up in your school community. First impressions are powerful, and a few minutes of your time may earn a friend and supporter for life. One principal makes sure that as guidance counselors give new parents and students a tour of the building, they find the principal and introduce the parents to the principal.

In addition to having packets of material ready for prospective parents, many schools provide an area in the office for displaying copies of materials and articles. These handouts keep parents and community members occupied if they have to wait, and they provide another source of positive public relations. Give the office secretary the responsibility of keeping the material current and in ample supply.

Many parents have specific questions about the curriculum, a specific course, or a special program. One way for a principal to have up-to-date information on each of these is to collect copies of the handouts each teacher gives to students or parents at the beginning of the year. With these, principals can create a notebook by department that can be updated each year. One principal has each department submit copies of the handouts given at Back to School Night. This creates an up-to-date curriculum and program guide.

- Create a school information packet for prospective parents.
- Use your office as a center for school handouts and information.
- Know your program and curriculum.

NOTE CARDS: THE BEST INVENTION SINCE SLICED BREAD

Note cards offer an abundance of uses for a principal. Keep a few blank ones in your pocket to jot down notes or reminders, to leave a note for someone, or to record inspirational quotes and ideas as they come to you for later development or filing.

Create a note card for each of your staff members, affixing a picture of the staff member to the card. Use the card to record notes about the staff member's background, interests, family, and so on. This is also a great transition tool. One new principal created a picture card for each staff member by making copies of a yearbook faculty section. She reviewed the cards so that she knew every staff member by name before starting the new job. She then held individual interviews with each staff member and kept notes on each card. Given the power of first impressions, her knowledge of names made a very positive first impression (see Resource C).

Note cards set up by educational topic can become a great interview preparation tool. One aspiring administrator built a set of more than one hundred topical cards based on interview questions and a review of current educational issues. The cards were easy to carry and could be reviewed as final preparation before an interview.

Principals are called on to speak at almost every school event, from formal ceremonies to informal gatherings. While preparing a detailed script for each event is ideal, practical necessity often means speaking extemporaneously. Having a collection of note cards on educational topics and with thoughtful quotes is a quick resource to draw on for remarks and speeches.

Note cards are also convenient for jotting down important reminders and notes. As a principal circulates around the school each day, staff and students often make a variety of requests. The principal can put each reminder on a separate note card; at the end of the day, the principal organizes the cards in priority order and thus has a quick way of organizing his or her work.

> - Learn the names of your students and staff members using picture note cards.
> - Note cards with quotes help make speeches easy.

THE MASTER KEY IS A MUST

Management by walking around was the rage in the 1990s. Books and articles touted the value of being visible on a regular basis. Effective principals instinctively knew this—practiced it, in fact—well before the concept became the business theme of the month. What good principals also know is how to make effective use of this walking-around time.

"Timing is everything" is a phrase that fits the principal's use of time. The start of the school day is a critical time for principals to be visible in the halls. On a practical level, principals see which staff members are ready to start and which arrive a few minutes late. Having your master key enables a principal to open the classrooms of late-arriving teachers and to clear the halls of students. Given the frequent shortage of available substitute teachers, the principal quickly becomes aware of any uncovered teacher absences and can take steps to resolve the problem.

Having a master key (or keys to all areas) is a must from a safety and security point of view. Often the principal is the first on the scene of a problem, and having access to appropriate equipment or locations is critical. A principal also needs to know the building and the essential systems that ensure safety and comfort. The fire alarm system, heating and ventilation system, intercom arrangement, phone system, and so on is essential for student and staff safety. Carrying a list of emergency phone numbers, access codes, keys, and so forth allows the principal to be an effective first responder to emergencies, no matter how small or great.

Many principals carry cell phones and pagers. Some cell phones can also function as walkie-talkies, thus providing two important functions. Program your cell phone with the important emergency and school numbers. Be sure your secretary and other key school personnel have your number.

Given the recent emphasis on emergency preparation and training, schools must have emergency plans, and often the principal maintains a special bag of emergency equipment in his or her office. This bag often contains a master list of students and staff, a list of phone numbers, a first-aid kit, and communication equipment, including a bullhorn and a mobile access device to the school's public address system.

- A master key not only opens doors, but it is also an essential emergency tool.
- Know your school's emergency systems.
- Prepare for the worst and do all you can to ensure the best.

STUDENT PLANNERS

Sometimes the best organizing systems are found right in front of you. Many schools purchase student planners for each student. Often these planners contain features that can help a busy administrator manage his or her time effectively.

Student planners can be custom designed to meet the needs of students, be a useful teaching and planning tool for faculty, and provide principals with a tool to unify the school. In addition, the planner also creates a way for students, faculty, and principals to more effectively manage time. Planners can also create a link between the parents, the students, and the school. Parents can be asked to review the planner periodically to note their child's assignments and to learn about upcoming events. The school can include material that was previously provided in handouts. For example, the school rules, graduation requirements, important telephone numbers, and so on can all be easily and inexpensively included in each planner (see Resource D).

Providing students and faculty with a planner also offers a principal the opportunity to engage representatives of each group in designing the planner. One principal uses his student leadership council to review such options as the size and format of the planners and any special features, such as reminder stickers, computer disk holders, and so on. Faculty input helps staff members buy in to the use of student planners.

As with many aspects of a school, the principal sets the tone. If the principal models the use of the planner, faculty and students are more likely to follow suit. The representatives of the companies that produce planners often have supplementary materials and programs available, sometimes at little or no cost. These run the gamut from character education materials to faculty workshops on how to help students be better organized.

As a principal, having all the key school rules and procedures in one place, a regular link to parents, and a unifying framework allows a principal to create and find more time to lead. The rapidly emerging world of electronic, handheld planners and computers permits even greater opportunities to improve communication and enhance organizational practices. Stay tuned for the amazing changes that the technology field will open for school administrators.

- Use student planners for many instructional purposes.
- Model appropriate use of planners.
- Involve students in designing the planner.
- Consolidate annual handouts into the planner.

Chapter Two

Time

There is never enough time to do it all and to do it right. This seems to be the mantra of an increasing number of principals. Every new piece of legislation, every court ruling, most parental concerns seem to require another study, another new program, or a change in practice. All of this takes time away from the reason that most principals took on the demands of the job—to make their school better for students and staff.

This chapter offers some practical tips on how principals can organize and use their time wisely. Careful planning and focusing on one's priorities and actions that reflect the underlying values of the job are critical to using one's time effectively.

BUILDING YOUR CALENDAR

Controlling your calendar is key. Too often principals find weeks go by without time for the priorities; each day becomes filled with meetings and events, with little or no time for visiting classes, doing research, or performing other tasks required of true leaders.

Begin by keeping your own calendar. Make your own appointments, including appointments to visit and observe classes and study quietly. You can easily accomplish this by using a pocket-size calendar and keeping it with you at all times. How many times has someone approached you in the hall or cafeteria and requested a meeting only to be told by you to see your secretary for an appointment? What a positive and efficient response it is to make that appointment on the spot. One principal keeps a small pad inside his calendar to make quick notes. He also maintains a comprehensive list of important phone numbers, which he updates each year on his computer and prints out to keep in his calendar.

Keeping your own calendar makes it harder for your secretary to make appointments for you, so keep your secretary updated on your calendar additions and changes each day. Also, have your secretary note when the person you are to meet is available and, after writing the appointment on your calendar, confirm with the person by e-mail or a phone call. In some cases, you may want to delegate all of your calendar responsibilities to your secretary. This requires effective communication and a secretary who understands your needs and priorities.

Now that you are making your own appointments, move from a reactive calendar to a proactive calendar. Begin each week by blocking out time to address your ongoing priorities and goals, rather than trying to catch time between meetings and appointments. A typical school week for middle and high schools is divided into periods. Make sure you monitor the number of periods you are devoting to priority issues. When you are able to devote at least one third of your week's school time to your major priorities, you have effectively gained control of your calendar. Your major priorities should include both formal and informal classroom observations, structured and unstructured time with students and parents, and time to lead that staff in meeting each of the goals the school has set for the year. One principal keeps a list of all faculty members in his calendar and records each informal visit. This helps him keep a useful record for the evaluation process and ensures all his staff members maintain contact with their principal.

Pocket-size calendars are easy to lose. Protect yourself against this by photocopying your calendar, much like you would back up your computer files. Keep your old calendars close by because they are a great source of information.

Modern technology has created the electronic calendar in the form of personal digital assistants. Some have enough memory and power to download a school's master schedule and student information. Some connect to a computer in the office, and others provide an e-mail option.

Maintaining a yearlong master calendar for the school can be a demanding task, given the multitude of activities, clubs, special events, and so on that a principal must keep track of. Take advantage of the many software packages for school administrators that include a calendar feature. Make all additions and changes in a timely manner and be sure to let all appropriate parties know. One principal uses a computer calendar program to print a list of all activities, meetings, and special events scheduled for the upcoming two-week period, which is then kept on an index card in the principal's pocket. The principal writes any additions or changes on the index card and later transcribes the changes onto the computer calendar program after he returns to the office. This helps him avoid embarrassing himself by showing up too early or late for a meeting, either in minutes, hours, days, or weeks.

Many principals keep a master calendar posted in the office. Just being able to visually see the schedule for the school year provides a good sense of the flow of events and meetings. It also enables other staff members to plan the date and time for programs and thus avoid scheduling conflicts. Another approach is to hold a weekly plant meeting, consisting of the head custodian, the kitchen director, the lead secretary, and the administrative team. The group reviews the past week's activities and discusses preparation for the coming week's calendar of events. This is also a great opportunity to keep all segments of the organization informed of issues around the school. Attention to detail and a dose of obsessive-compulsiveness will prevent wasted time and calendar conflicts.

> - Keep your own calendar.
> - Be proactive with your calendar.
> - Be obsessive about your calendar; make it public and avoid conflicts.

BEING IN TWO PLACES AT ONCE

The demands on a principal's time can be overwhelming. From a never-ending series of district meetings to afternoon, evening, and weekend events, principals are in constant demand. The symbolic responsibilities of the role make it imperative to be at almost every major activity and at some of each club's, sport's, and group's events, games, or programs. Getting your day-to-day work done and attending to all of these responsibilities is near impossible.

Some principals have discovered that they do not have to attend events for the full duration. Be visible at the beginning of the event, and, once it is underway, you can slip out, either to get some much needed time at home or to push the paperwork ahead undisturbed in your office. You can also arrive late for an event or take a break from your work to attend the intermission or the conclusion of the event.

If you have assistant principals or other administrative team members, share the responsibility of supervising and attending events. A few minutes of coordinating calendars helps ensure that every group feels supported by the administration.

Principals frequently end up with conflicting events that demand their presence and attention. Rather than picking one over another, attend part of each event.

> - Share and coordinate attendance at student events.
> - Spend a little time at a lot of events.

Your many constituencies will appreciate your appearance at part of the event. This is one time that less is really more.

MEETINGS

Principals too often find their days filled with meetings. Everyone from the superintendent to the student government wants the principal on his or her committee. Many times principals are their own worst enemies. They create structures and practices that fill each day with meetings they initiated. When combined with all the other expectations and demands of being instructional and educational leader and manager, too many meetings create isolation and detachment from the daily life of a school.

Principals should keep meetings to a minimum. Make sure agendas are carefully planned and distributed to all parties in advance. The agenda should be divided into sections for information items and action items to help expedite meetings. Cancel those standing meetings when there are no pressing agenda items. Your faculty will appreciate such efforts.

Running an effective meeting is truly an art. Participants want the opportunity to be heard but also want issues to be processed in a timely manner. Knowing when to call for closure, forging consensus, and recognizing when to drop an item are very important skills. Start and end on time and be sensitive to the mood and tone of the group. Many how-to books about meetings are available, but it is just as effective to solicit feedback from those who attend your meetings.

Principals not only have to run a lot of meetings, but they also have to attend many, which can be quite time-consuming. Some meeting topics demand a principal's full attention. The annual budget process meeting with the central office is critical to ensure your school and its staff members get their fair share of the budget pie. On the other hand, meetings to review the district's policy manual or to consider the cafeteria menu are frequently boring and always seem to drag on forever. Rather than day dreaming, use the time productively by writing a memo or updating your lists or schedule. In short, be sure to bring paperwork with you but do it in a circumspect way so as not to insult the meeting chairperson. (See the section "Carry Your Desk With You" in Chapter 1 for strategies to help you keep all of your immediate work on hand at all times.)

Meetings should and can be a place to build camaraderie and support for your school's culture and vision. One principal begins every meeting with a discussion of a short article sent out in advance of the meeting, along with the agenda. The article is carefully selected to keep staff members focused on the overall vision of the school. This principal also closes each meeting with an around-the-table exercise, giving each person the opportunity to reflect on the issues they feel are important. Creating such a pattern provides not only structure but also a tone that helps move meetings along and makes them worthwhile.

- Keep meetings short and to the point.
- Listen for the consensus and recognize when to call for closure.
- Build routines into meetings to nourish the school's culture.
- Celebrate and give positive feedback often.

GETTING STARTED

The best way to get started each morning is to prepare for it the day before. Taking ten minutes before you leave at the end of the day to preview the schedule for the coming day goes far in making your mornings go smoothly.

End each day by preparing the materials, backup folders, and other supplies you need for the next day. When you arrive in the morning, make a quick tour of the building and touch base with your custodial staff to be sure all is in order. Then check the status of teacher illnesses and the availability of substitutes. Be ready to step into the breach and cover a homeroom or class until a substitute or another teacher arrives. Take advantage of the contact with students to find out which issues or concerns are on their minds.

Early mornings are often a good time to schedule parent conferences. In most cases, you have a built-in time limit for morning conferences because parents must head off to work. Mornings also provide principals with a chance to informally chat with students and staff. Take a few minutes to mingle with arriving students or drink your morning coffee in a department office rather than at your desk.

Communication with your secretary is critical in the morning. Emergencies and problems usually come to the secretary's attention first. Make sure you can be reached anywhere in the building. A good communication system—either by pager, walkie-talkie, or cell phone—takes care of this need.

Scheduling committee meetings before school creates a fixed ending time because committee members must get to classes. Providing coffee and refreshments helps get the participants to the meeting on time.

- Begin each day the night before.
- Schedule parent conferences to fit parent schedules.
- Feed your staff at meetings.
- Maintain a good communication system.

COFFEE SHOP TIME

Finding uninterrupted time to complete pressing reports or to do some sustained reading is very difficult. Closing your door and asking your secretary to hold your calls does not work given the frequent emergencies that quickly end up in your hands if you are in the building.

Principals need to build time into their schedules to work and think in a quiet and secluded environment. For some, it may mean Saturday mornings in the office with no phone calls or family. For others, it may be a quick trip to an area park or library. One busy principal makes his neighborhood coffee shop his afternoon stop. In an hour over a cup of coffee, he dispenses with the mail, writes memos, and organizes materials for the coming day. The stop also serves as a transition from work to home, enabling him to arrive home ready to give his full attention to family responsibilities and needs.

- Create opportunities for uninterrupted work time.
- Make a smooth transition from work to home.
- Use time to ensure your own needs are attended to.

There is no one answer to the need for quiet time; each principal needs to assess his or her own patterns and find a practice that works. Much of becoming an effective leader comes from self-awareness and personal growth.

TELEPHONE TIME

The telephone is a vital tool for a principal, given the busy lives so many parents and staff members lead. Even so, the telephone can become an annoying source of interruptions and can create inefficiency if not managed carefully.

When using the phone, office staff should reflect the tone and professionalism of your school. Greetings should be upbeat and should invite callers to share their concerns or questions. Staff should screen calls, routing callers to the most appropriate staff member. Those calls that the principal must handle should be prioritized, and detailed messages should be secured by the office staff. As principal, establish regular times to return your calls and prioritize them, so you make the most problematic calls when you have sufficient time and patience to process the issues at hand.

Many schools have sophisticated phone systems that include voice mail, both individually and by groupings, as well as automated answering and routing of calls. Be sure to involve parents when you adopt such a system to maintain the personalization and user efficiency wanted by the parents. All too often automated systems damage public relations and school community relationships if careful attention and sensitivity is ignored.

One local principal saves all telephone message slips in special folders. These become part of the archives, which help in numerous situations, from responding to lawsuits to finding a phone number that no one else has. An effective alternative is to use a carbon paper message book. Keeping a telephone logbook is another strategy some principals use. This system involves a written log that includes space for notes on each call and is organized by date and time. Voice mail is another handy method for archiving messages. Voice mail contains a memory system that lets you save messages for years.

Principals should be proactive in the use of phones. Specifically, make time to call parents or staff members to congratulate them on important accomplishments. Encourage your staff to send you notes to make such calls. In short, you become a role model for a practice you would like all of your teachers to follow.

Early mornings and evenings often provide quality time for phone calls. Cell phone technology gives principals the flexibility to make calls at any time and from any place.

- Efficient use of the phone saves a great deal of time.
- Involve all constituents in the selection of a new phone system.
- Keep records of both incoming and outgoing calls.
- Encourage staff members to call parents often by making phones accessible.

SAVE YOUR CALENDARS

Schools are creatures of habit. School patterns and routines are predictable and resistant to change. Building and maintaining a school calendar that includes time for the hundreds of programs, activities, and meetings that every school has takes careful planning and a bit of creative license. Once your school has a calendar system that works, keep it.

Principals can save a great deal of time by simply replicating the yearly calendar of events. Save each year's calendar and use it to build the next. Make notes on the calendar so that when you review for the following year the information is right at your fingertips. Recognize that any change may have a domino effect, so be sure to look at the big picture before moving or adding an event.

A file of past years' calendars is also a great source of information. Look at how your time as a principal was allocated. Calculate how much time you spent in classrooms, in meetings, doing paperwork, and meeting with parents. This information can become a baseline from which you can set time-management priorities.

Past calendars also serve as an historical record that you may need for a variety of reasons. More schools and principals face legal challenges. Being able to identify the dates and times of meetings can help fill in a picture that all too often fades from memory almost as soon as it is over. Another use for calendars involves expense logs. Many districts reimburse administrators for mileage to and from school events. The calendar offers a quick and simple record of out-of-district meetings and events.

> • Calendars are a great way to track your use of time.
> • Build next year's school calendar by starting with this year's.
> • Create a file of previous years' calendars.

ACCREDITATION

Many schools across the country are accredited by regional independent agencies. In the past, the accreditation process was primarily a high school practice, but in recent years elementary and middle schools have joined in the process. In fact, the Middle States Association of Colleges and Schools reports that its fastest growing area of accreditation is a K–12, districtwide process that includes every school in the district.

Accreditation can be a very time-consuming and stressful process that more often than not falls on the shoulders of the principal. One of the keys to managing the process is to make it part of the overall school program. In this way, accreditation helps accomplish work that would be needed anyway. In other words, incorporate the demands of the accreditation process into the tasks that have to be completed. Even more important, effective principals often use the process to address needs that have otherwise been difficult to approach.

Creating time in a principal's and a school's already crowded schedule to complete the accreditation process presents an opportunity to create time for productive dialogue among all constituents of the school community. For example, one principal was able to convince the district to hold a series of delayed starts for students to carve out extended time for faculty to address the tasks required by accreditation. The morning workshops were so successful that they became a regular part of the school's calendar. The extra work time has also energized faculty by giving them time to work on important issues at the most productive time of the day.

> • Make accreditation a part of your school's regular program.
> • Use accreditation as a means to secure needed improvements and resources.
> • Encourage staff members to serve as members of accreditation teams.

Accreditation is also a process that provides the principal with a great deal of support and structure. The accrediting agencies offer a variety of workshops and materials that can be used in any improvement process. The agencies also have experienced staff members, many of whom are former principals, who can serve as a valuable resource.

Chapter Three

Communication

The ability to effectively communicate with all school community members can mean the difference between an average principal and one who is very effective. A less than effective communicator treads water all day, going back and forth between groups, trying to solve problems but never reaching a solution. Principals need to communicate their vision and goals using clear language that people will understand and, hopefully, embrace as their own. As a principal, you need to be proactive about everything you do, anticipating and defusing problems before they escalate into crises. A principal who is a good communicator gives a sense of security to his or her staff, students, and parents.

Principals should teach those around them by example, modeling how to be effective communicators. When everyone hears and buys in to the principal's view of communication, an environment is created where misunderstandings, problems, and wasted time are drastically reduced.

HOW TO USE A TELEPHONE

It is important to return phone calls as soon as possible. You may want to set aside a time, preferably in the morning, to return most calls. A quick response to a phone call can often solve a small problem before it becomes a big issue. If you anticipate a problem with the person who called, gather from staff any information about why the person may have called. This research enables you to be better prepared and more able to solve a problem or confront a negative situation. When someone calls, have your secretary ask the caller the reason for the call. This often gives a principal the added information he or she needs to more aptly solve problems.

Principals need to be good listeners if they are to solve problems in a logical and fair manner. Let callers talk without interruption and make them feel assured that what they are saying is important. Listening to a caller does not guarantee that you will take an action that you aren't sure of or that you don't agree with.

Since you want to conserve time on the phone, if a conversation doesn't seem to be going anywhere or accomplishing a great deal, suggest a face-to-face meeting. When it comes to phone conversations, short calls are almost always more productive than long ones. Reassure the caller that you will look into the matter of concern, then look into it quickly and get back to the caller.

- Gather data.
- Be a good listener.
- Make phone calls short.
- Follow through.

VISIBILITY: LEADING BY WALKING AROUND

Being seen by the school community on a daily basis is as important as what you say at meetings or in memos. Principals who walk through the building, talking with staff and students give the members of their team a sense of security and purpose. A principal's visible presence on a regular basis adds validity to the work that the teachers are doing.

When planning your day, you might want to select a designated area of the building to spend a definitive period of time. Talk informally with staff before school starts and spend time formally observing and talking to students in that designated area. By setting aside a specific time and area in your plan book or computer calendar, you avoid wandering throughout the building, which often needlessly occupies a principal's limited time.

Each day, change the designated area to visit so that you spend a block of time in all areas of the building each week. One principal picked a grade level area to visit, to ensure consistency.

Showing the staff your human side is an important means of communication and can help to enhance the lines of communication when dealing with professional issues. One effective approach is to walk around the building before students arrive and informally chat with staff members who may be in their rooms or in the halls. Asking staff about their families, their hobbies, or anything related to their out-of-school experiences shows them that you care about them as fellow human beings, not just as hired employees. Often staff members will ask you a question during this time that can be answered on the spot. These questions would take much more time to answer if they were asked at scheduled meetings or in your office, diminishing everyone's valuable time. It's best to provide answers to these quick questions if possible to avoid wasting time in meetings.

There are innumerable reasons why the students and parents need to physically see the principal on a regular basis. The students enjoy seeing you—the educational leader of their school—in their classrooms, showing an interest in the work that they are accomplishing. Parents feel that they have left you in charge of their children, and when they see you on a regular basis they gain confidence that their children are in good hands when they are away from home.

- Walk around the building each day.
- Target specific areas to visit.
- Show your informal, human side.

THE WORKING LUNCH

It is a rare occasion when a principal has an uninterrupted lunchtime. Some principals find it helpful to schedule regular working lunches with a variety of groups within the school community. Include teachers, students, parents, and support staff in these working lunches. All of these groups have one thing in common—they all enjoy eating!

When possible, use district money to provide pizza or sandwiches for small informal group meetings with you. If this is not possible, hold bring-your-own-lunch meetings, where you provide the beverages and dessert. These lunches should not be formal affairs; rather, they should be opportunities for the members of the school community to have a casual meeting with the principal in his or her office.

One principal started informal lunch meetings by announcing a volunteer lunchtime at a faculty meeting and was pleasantly surprised by the overwhelming support for such a concept. Often entire grade levels, special programs staff, students, and parents are eager to sign up for lunch with the principal.

These lunch meetings are invaluable in encouraging everyone in the school community to communicate with you. Remember that you want to know everything that is going on in your building, and you will be amazed by how much people open up in this informal setting. This is a perfect opportunity for a relaxed sharing of ideas and gives you insights into the people you work with that you may miss while observing or walking around the building.

As the educational leader of the building and the role model for communication, you can reap tremendous rewards from these lunchtime meetings.

People open up more when they see you in these informal settings, and they share many positive things about the school community.

Don't be surprised if some members of the lunch meeting do not talk at first. They will open up as soon as they see the meeting as nonthreatening and hear the other members talking. Remember, this is their meeting, so be a good listener and limit your advice and input. Make sure to send a short, handwritten note thanking everyone for participating.

Because of time constraints, hosting these lunches every two or three weeks is more than enough. In that time, you can include everyone interested in attending. Some principals host Coffee with the Principal, which is a meeting that helps keep the lines of communication open.

- Host several small group lunches.
- Relax and share ideas.
- Don't take physical notes; take mental notes.

PARENTS AS PARTNERS

The support of the parent community is essential to your goal as an effective principal. Parental support can be gained by communicating often and clearly with parents. This communication takes a variety of forms and should include regular letters home, phone calls to parents for a variety of reasons, and visibility and speaking at parent-teacher activities. As the principal, you need to clearly explain to parents what your philosophy of education is and how you will ensure the safety and educational development of their children.

It is imperative for you to be visible and available to parents because you are the guardian of their children while they are away from home. No parent concern should be taken lightly, and by addressing parent concerns as soon as possible you quickly begin to be seen by parents as someone who cares about their children, a person with a willingness to communicate with the parent community.

Although it is human to like some parents more than others, it is important to be seen as fair and equitable, not biased toward any one group of constituents. Remember that all parents are stakeholders in your organization and that their own children are the children they care most about. Make sure when you meet with parents that you are not distracted with other responsibilities and reassure them that you are very willing and open to talk about their concerns.

Effectively communicating with parents prevents rumors that are often difficult to eliminate. Remind parents that they should contact you if they hear anything that disturbs or concerns them. Encourage them to avoid listening to other parents' complaints and to call you as soon as a concern develops. This approach often eliminates destructive and often inaccurate information from spreading throughout the community.

In the same manner, you teach good communication skills to staff by being a good communicator. Model openness and honesty with parents. If you or someone on staff makes a mistake (and this does happen), be straightforward about it and offer a way to correct the situation. Trying to avoid communication for a period of time only adds complexity to an often simple solution.

- Use a variety of communication venues.
- Don't play favorites.
- Dispel rumors.
- Be open and honest.

PUBLIC PRESENTATIONS

When you get the opportunity to speak in front of a group, large or small, be prepared. These meetings should be viewed as opportunities to better explain your philosophy and to reaffirm for parents that their children's safety and social and educational development are your paramount concern.

You may want to keep a daily log on your computer that briefly outlines each day's activities. When you need to develop a presentation, you can refer to your log for an outline of the core of your speech. The log helps you to remember past events that may be of importance to parents. It is also useful for developing an agenda for a faculty or grade-level meeting.

As you begin to formulate your thoughts, remember that parents want to hear what their children are doing in school. Activities that are routine for a principal or teacher are always new and exciting for parents, especially when the activity directly affects their children.

Always build in time for a question-and-answer session in your presentation, encouraging a two-way street in the communication process. Although principals should make every effort to know as much as possible about their buildings, it is impossible to know everything. If you cannot answer a parent's question immediately, assure the parent that you will find the answer and get back to him or her with the information. Then make sure you get back with the answer as soon as possible. Not knowing the answer to everything is not a problem; not responding with the answer in a timely fashion is a problem.

- Keep a daily log.
- Be specific, citing real examples.
- Target the members of the audience.

Chapter Four

Delegation

It is impossible for a principal to do everything or be everywhere to oversee all of the operations of a building on any given day. If you are going to be an effective and efficient administrator, you must learn how to be a good delegator. This does not mean simply assigning tasks or giving people chores that you don't feel like doing. True delegation involves stating your goals for specific people or groups (e.g., custodians, secretaries), assigning them a task, and then giving them the time, space, and support they need to carry out those tasks in a productive manner.

QUESTIONS TO ASK

If delegation is to have lasting, productive results, the principal must do a great deal of planning. Principals needs to ask themselves a series of questions:

1. What is the job I want accomplished?
2. Who is best suited to accomplish this task?
3. Is it easier to just do the task myself?
4. How will I define the task to the person selected?
5. What information will I need to give this person so he or she can accomplish the task successfully?
6. How much time will I give the person to accomplish the task?
7. How will we assess the success of the task?

- Delegation gives the principal valuable time and empowers staff.
- Plan delegation well before floating the offer.
- Delegation creates leaders among the staff.

Delegation has long-term positive effects if it's done well: Not only is the task accomplished, but also a sense of leadership and importance is given to the person assigned the task. Delegation creates teams among staff members and can be a valuable tool in creating a united front for the vision of a leader.

USE YOUR STAFF

As the principal, whom you give responsibilities to is your decision. An effective principal quickly realizes that everyone in the school community is capable and willing to carry out some task and that by delegating tasks the leader creates leaders among the entire school community. Whether it is a custodian who has a strong interest in woodworking and builds showcases to hold school awards or a secretary who enjoys organizing faculty parties, staff members have varied talents, and an effective principal quickly learns to identify and make use of these interests and talents.

The number and type of personnel available to a principal varies according to each school. While the following sections refer to some of the more common school structures, you should realize that everyone in the building and school community is able to carry out tasks that you might assign them. Most will accept the challenge willingly!

- Give everyone the opportunity for responsibility.
- Most people will accept challenges.
- Learn the interests and talents of the staff.

Custodians

While the primary goal of a custodian is to keep a building clean, the principal can delegate special tasks to custodians that are important to the proper running of the school, while making the employee feel like more than just someone who cleans up after everyone.

One task we have given custodians is to greet the parents in the morning as they drop their children off in the parking lot. This gives custodians a sense of responsibility for the safe arrival of children and creates a link between the parent community and the custodial staff. It shows the parents, staff, and students that the principal values the custodians not only as cleaners but also as people who have direct, positive contact with the children. Delegating this responsibility to the custodians instilled a sense of leadership among them and allowed us more time to work on other tasks.

At least once a week, walk through the area assigned to the custodians to make sure that things are moving smoothly. Do not do this every day because you want the custodians to know that you trust their ability to accomplish their tasks. When we did this, we were pleasantly surprised to see how seriously the custodians took their tasks and the real sense of pride they got from their accomplishments.

> - Extend everyone's responsibility to increase ownership.
> - Delegate, provide support, stand back and observe.

Secretaries

Secretaries are probably the most powerful people in a school hierarchy after the principal. They are on the front line for everything that goes on in a building. As a principal, you know how important secretaries are for the efficient running of the school. If you don't know this, you will quickly learn it when things begin to go awry.

It is important for you to ensure that your secretaries feel empowered and important. You need to delegate to them certain responsibilities beyond their expected secretarial duties.

Every few months, meet with secretaries on an individual basis and then with them as a group. During these meetings, ask how things are going and try to impress upon them how important they are you and to the school community. If you can develop a strong bond between you and them, you will have a friend who will inform you of things that you may not otherwise be privy to.

Delegate tasks to the secretaries that will give them a feeling of leadership. Many of the tasks that we have assigned our secretaries involve the tone and atmosphere of the school, which we want to extend throughout the building.

Because secretaries are often the first person people have contact with, delegate to them the authority to ask people why they want to meet with you. Done in a friendly and appropriate manner, this inquiry usually explains why someone is coming in and also allows you to gather appropriate data before the meeting. This simple task will help you to be more efficient and prepared.

You can also put secretaries in charge of committees in the sense that they organize the members, establish dates for meetings, and see these committees through from conception to completion. While they are not usually members of the committee (although you can make the secretaries committee members when appropriate), secretaries feel a sense of ownership with the members of the committee and the staff. When the operation of a committee goes smoothly,

- After the principal, the secretary is the second person on the front line.
- Show the staff how much you value the secretaries.
- Make the secretaries an integral part of the school community team.

this sense of ownership is valuable for the next time a committee needs to be formed and organized.

Teacher-Leaders

Most schools have teachers whose job it is to make sure that their grade-level colleagues have all of the supplies that they need and are current on curriculum areas. A principal who is aware of the benefits of delegation uses these people wisely to accomplish the goals of the building.

Meet with these teacher-leaders twice a month and always have specific tasks for them to accomplish. After explaining the benefit of what you want to accomplish, make sure that the teacher-leaders are in agreement with you and let them know how much you value their leadership.

- Turn grade-level leaders into spokespeople for your vision.
- As leaders with special responsibilities, grade-level leaders take on new ownership.
- By using grade-level leaders to spread your word, you guarantee that the entire staff gets the message.

These team leaders then go back to their colleagues, and your word is spread among the faculty in a short period of time. Having these people working as leaders gives them a sense of responsibility and pride and saves you a tremendous amount of time. The time saved can certainly be used efficiently to accomplish the many tasks a principal needs to perform.

Parents

There are always groups of parents who are more than willing to take on tasks that benefit their own children and the school as a community. Use the enthusiasm of these people by delegating to them various tasks related to the school. For example, one principal used parent volunteers to decorate and landscape a newly created courtyard after their building was expanded. Another principal empowers the parents of high school students to plan and run an end-of-year graduation party. One district uses parent volunteer to maintain a parenting center, which provides information and resources on a variety of parent issues to the community.

The PTA should be empowered with more than running bake sales. By involving the PTA in important issues (curriculum, policy making, etc.), you provide the school with an additional source of support. Many parent-teacher organizations have incredible fundraising power. The more the principal stays involved with the organization, the more likely the principal will have significant input into how the money will be used.

> • Parents are always eager to help; use this enthusiasm to drum up support for important issues.
> • Empower appropriate and capable parents with important tasks.

FACULTY MEETINGS CAN BE FUN

Faculty meetings are great opportunities to delegate responsibilities to members of the staff. When possible, this kind of delegation should be accomplished by asking for volunteers. Whatever the task, it should first be explained thoroughly to the staff so that interested people volunteer for the project.

We have found that teachers are more willing to volunteer for additional tasks if they can work with some of their colleagues. This is why a faculty meeting provides a great venue for people to volunteer as teams.

By delegating responsibilities to various members of the school community, you accomplish two main goals: You free yourself up to work on other tasks, and you empower people to accomplish tasks that will benefit your school and give the professionals a true sense of accomplishment in areas outside the classroom.

> • Delegation provides the principal with time to attend to other tasks.
> • Delegation empowers staff members.
> • Everyone in the school community can take on additional responsibilities.
> • Once you assign someone a task, give the person the time and resources to accomplish the task.

Chapter Five

Summer

Depending on district and administrative contracts, principals typically work, officially, ten or eleven months a year. In reality, principals are year-round employees. Many principals never take their full vacation because there are always surprises and unexpected events that occur during the summer that need the personal attention of the building principal. These unexpected events usually include staff resignations or illnesses, enrollment increases, structural problems with the building, and interviews for additional staff positions that you didn't count on having to fill.

Summer provides valuable time for a principal and lacks the intensity and fast pace of the regular school year. Used wisely, this time can help principals create a smoother opening to school in September and help in the general running of the school throughout the year.

STAFF SELECTION

Staff selection is one of the most important tasks of a principal. In many cases, it is a million dollar decision because more often than not the person hired stays with the school for his or her entire career. The earlier in the year you can start the hiring process, the better. By conducting interviews early in the summer, you gain the availability of your teachers to serve on interview committees, and you gain time for the best candidates to be brought back to teach demonstration lessons. Some principals make it a practice to see the teacher candidates who currently hold teaching positions teach in their current setting rather than teach a demonstration lesson. Most new staff members are hired during the summer. At the last two faculty meetings of the year, ask for staff volunteers to serve on a staff selection committee during the summer. Principals should appreciate the value of shared decision making and should develop a list of staff members who are willing to give of their time. We are always amazed and pleasantly surprised at how many staff members take this responsibility seriously and are willing to give of their vacation time. Once committed, the staff selection committee does its best to hire quality staff because the reputations of the committee members are at issue.

- Ask for volunteers for interview committees long before the end of the school year.
- Value the volunteers and the time they are giving.
- New staff members hired by committees are usually of the highest quality.

Doing telephone reference checks as a final step before hiring is also crucial. While some laws and district practices make telephone reference checks difficult, a response of "I'm not able to answer" or " I have no comment" from a previous supervisor can be telling.

SAVE THOSE RESUMES

It is a good idea to number and save resumes as they come into the office. One principal has his secretaries keep resumes filed in the order in which they were received, in groups of twenty-five. As the resumes come in during the year, the secretaries place them in files. The files are boxed and stored for future reference.

When you form your staff selection committee, each member can take a certain number of resumes to review and select those that they feel the rest of the team would be interested in reviewing. It is important that you take the time to read all of the resumes and that you make sure the team knows the importance of reading resumes. Once all of the resumes have been read, the committee comes together to create one master list of candidates whom they wish to interview. We have always made known that both an interview and a demonstration lesson are required of the candidates we are considering for teaching positions. We require demonstration lessons because some people are very good during the interview process but are not good with children. Using this process of shared decision making gives you the time to review any or all of the resumes and make personal calls to local universities and colleges to see if they know of highly qualified candidates who have recently graduated. Often the education department at local colleges is an excellent resource for referrals of qualified young teachers.

Another source of qualified candidates are the students teachers in your building. When working with student teachers, you not only have a firsthand opportunity to observe and develop quality candidates, but also your own teachers gain the positive professional development experience of mentoring a student teacher.

> • Value staff members who volunteer to work on summer committees.
> • Shared decision making, well planned, makes the school community a stronger and more productive unit.
> • Local colleges and universities are a good source of quality candidates.

STUDENT PLACEMENT RECORDS

The summer is a good time for you to review student records, which allows you to see the progress being made by individual students. You can also see how individual classes are doing, compared with other classes on the same grade level. Are there marked differences among the classes? Does there seem to be a pattern of students doing poorly in any one class? Does it seem that all of the classes are pretty similar with regard to test results? If the answer to any of these questions is yes, the principal should take it as a sign that more data need to be reviewed to find any patterns that may need to be addressed.

These placement records can also help teachers improve their teaching. Have teachers review data from their classrooms and formulate a self-assessment of their strengths and areas in need of improvement. This process also creates an historical record that can be used for both student development and teacher effectiveness.

> • Review student records for trends.
> • Follow student patterns from one grade to the next and from one teacher to the next.

STUDENT PLACEMENT PROCEDURES

Student placement is an important process that helps the school year get off to a positive start. When possible, student placement is best accomplished during the summer because it allows the principal the time and flexibility necessary to divide classes equitably and fairly. Student placement, when possible, is best accomplished when a team of staff members makes placements that are in both the interest of the student and the teacher. We have developed a procedure with our staff that takes into consideration a variety of factors when placing children in the next grade. We and our staff assess and fine-tune the procedure every year and have what we consider a very fine set of procedures for student placement. Below is a brief outline of our procedure for student placement:

1.   Teachers separate their current students into the classes for the next year. This is done in May or June, just before the school year ends. The teachers try to balance each class, taking into consideration the numbers of girls and boys, the students with behavioral problems and reading abilities, the students' home locations in town, any personal conflicts students might have with each other, and ethnicity and home languages.

2.   Receiving teachers look at these classes and make changes if they see any issues, such as teachers having taught siblings or having problems in the past with specific families.

3.   Specialists and teachers of special programs are then invited to look at the lists.

4.   The principal randomly puts the names of the teachers at the top of the completed class lists. It is agreed on prior to final placement that the principal has the ability to change any student placement where he or she deems necessary.

During the summer, principals review the classes to try to ensure, as much as possible, that the classes start off equitably and that there are few major problems at the opening of school. The process described previously has been extremely successful in establishing classes that are heterogeneous and balanced across the grade level.

Some principals involve parents in the student placement process as well. One principal has parents fill out a consideration form but includes a disclaimer that the school has the final say in student assignment. One high school has a written policy for student placement that allows parents to request teacher changes if a sibling had the teacher and did poorly, for example, or if the student had the teacher before and failed. The policy also provides a catch-all step, whereby the school psychologist may recommend a change if a serious personality conflict exists.

> - Involve all in placement decisions.
> - Keep the process as objective as possible.
> - Provide avenues for parent input.

KEEPING YOUR FILES ACTIVE

The summer is an excellent time for updating, deleting, and organizing files from the previous school year. We have learned from past experience that it is valuable to set up a summer to-do file in March, which helps us to be more organized during the summer as we begin to get ready for the coming school year.

From March until June, keep a running list of things that are important for next year but that do not need immediate attention until summer. This list could include things such as room changes, student test results, speakers for next year's assemblies, faculty and grade-level meeting dates, and a wide variety of things that can best be accomplished during the summer when the days are less hectic.

- Organize and read files you didn't have time to review during the year.
- Use a summer to-do list to establish goals and objectives for the upcoming school year.

GETTING READY FOR THE YEAR

A good way to help ensure a smooth opening to each school year is to invite a variety of parents in to meet with you during the summer. Provide some form of refreshment during these meetings and use the time to review the past year with the parent community and to elicit their suggestions for the year to come.

Parents view these invitations as a sign of goodwill and an honest request for their input. These meetings are invaluable in their ability to help establish new or refined procedures for the following school year. Since parents feel comfortable to share their thoughts during these meetings, you will hear helpful information that otherwise you would probably never know had you not provided these informal sessions. Parents feel comfortable sharing their thoughts and concerns, and we have found that the meetings are usually positive in nature and do not become gripe sessions. At the beginning of each of these parent meetings, make sure to set the ground rules for the discussions, which are simply that everyone is at the meeting to promote positive changes and or modifications for the following year, that no discussion of personnel is allowed, and that a free exchange of ideas is always encouraged.

Some principals find periodic surveys of parents a good method for assessing programs and practices. There are many commercially available survey instruments that can be used or modified to meet a particular school's situation.

- Meet with parents during the summer to ensure a smoother opening to the next school year.
- Plan parent meetings well to establish guidelines, direction, and outcomes.
- Staff members enjoy the informal time you give them during the summer.

During the summer, take the time to meet with staff members who come to the school for a variety of reasons. Most teachers come to organize their rooms and to prepare for the coming year. When possible, form focus groups with these teachers, luring them in with a promise of a pizza lunch. A great deal is accomplished during these informal summer lunch meetings, and the teachers learn that, if they come in during the summer, they can give their somewhat private input to you, who, in return, will feed them!

REMEMBER YOUR OWN PROFESSIONAL DEVELOPMENT

The daily life of a principal is full of obligations and responsibilities, always for the well-being of others and the improvement and smooth running of the school. As a result, principals often overlook the need to continue their growth as professionals. Time captured during the summer should involve a focus on the principal's own professional development and improvement.

Many colleges offer some type of principal forum during the summer. These are usually valuable workshops where administrators exchange ideas, beliefs, and thoughts about best practice. These workshops give principals a sense of being part of a bigger picture, and we have found them to be a source of revitalization at the end of a long year. Taking a graduate course or attending a professional conference are also great ways to recharge one's batteries and to gain up-to-date information and knowledge. Most counties have administrative organizations, often with a chapter devoted just for elementary, middle, and high school principals. These groups offer support and current information and can serve as an advocacy group with the state and county departments of education. The principalship can be very lonely without support.

Don't forget to keep abreast of the current literature on leadership because the definition and direction for school leadership changes regularly. By reading the current research on leadership and attending collegial groups or seminars during the summer, you better prepare yourself for the coming school year.

- Take the time to stay current.
- Attend administrative seminars and collegial circles.
- Keeping up with the current literature on leadership and teaching has positive effects on your performance and the performance of your staff.

Chapter Six

People

To be a successful principal, you have to be a real, sincere people person. If a principal is to be effective, he or she must like people, be willing to try to understand where each member of the team is coming from, and be willing and eager to find out about each person as an individual. If you do not have a people-oriented personality, being a school principal is probably not the profession for you. Staff members quickly recognize principals who are not truly interested in them and are reluctant to go along with the principals' goals and objectives.

KNOW YOUR FACULTY AND STAFF

As the principal and leader of a school, one of your major responsibilities is to get to know your faculty and staff as individuals. You need to understand and internalize that, like you, they are following their chosen profession as best they can, and they are looking to you for guidance, support, and encouragement. Take the time to find out about each staff member and show that you appreciate him or her as both a professional and as a person.

Get to know your faculty members' families and ask about them on a regular basis. Make sure to keep abreast of marriages, illnesses, and how staff members' children are doing in school or in their chosen careers. We often walk around our building in the morning and catch up on the other-than-school news with a few staff members each day. Using a staff roster, we keep track of those staff members whom we have spoken with each day to ensure that we touch base with every staff member, informally, at least once a week.

As mentioned previously, unless you genuinely like and care about people, your sincerity or lack thereof will come through quickly. We know several former administrators who never made it in the field because they really weren't people oriented. They weren't up to the challenge of putting in the time required to really get to know the people they worked with to earn their confidence and support.

An effective way to encourage and support people is to recognize them in public. A great forum for this recognition is a faculty or PTA meeting. Staff members' accomplishments or milestones—and those of their families—are worthy of recognition. Your faculty meeting is a perfect venue for this kind of recognition. While many faculty members say they don't feel comfortable being praised in front of their peers, in reality everyone enjoys being recognized.

- Take the time to really listen to and get to know staff.
- Be visible and available to staff before and after school.
- Publicly recognize staff members for their achievements and milestones.
- Show by your actions and words that you are interested in your staff members and their families.

LEARN THOSE STUDENT NAMES

Everyone likes to hear his or hear name, and students are especially thrilled when the principal calls them by their name. This is especially true when the student isn't in trouble. Learning names, especially with a large student population, is not an easy task for a principal. Accomplishing this task requires concentration and time. As difficult as remembering so many names may be at times, one of the benefits of learning students' names is having students who know that you care about them as individuals. This helps greatly to create an atmosphere of mutual trust and respect between the principal and the student body.

Over the years, we have asked for staff support in helping us to learn student names. For at least the first few weeks of school, we ask the staff to put students' first and last names on their desks. We then spend time in classrooms, trying to match names with faces. In about a month's time, we learn approximately 80% of the students' names. We ask the other 20% when we see them in the lunchroom or around the building. Another way to learn names is to keep a picture of each class with names in your office and to review it on a regular basis.

We often stand in the lunchroom after a few weeks and try to name each child. Although this is a time-consuming project, the task truly pays off when within the first few weeks of the school year you can call all students by name when you say hello, something that honors and surprises the students.

At the middle and high school levels, a successful method for learning names is to give everyone in the building a nametag for at least the first week of school. Not only does this allow the principal to begin learning names, but it also gives the students a way to make new friends and become familiar with the names of the entire school community.

Encouraging everyone in the building to wear nametags at the beginning of the year fosters a feeling of community where all constituents feel part of the same team.

- A name has great value to a person.
- Take the time to match names with faces.
- Surprise students in the hall by calling them by name.

BREAK BREAD TOGETHER

One of the best ways to get to know the students' names and to get to know them as individuals is to have lunch with them. Select one day a month to have lunch with each of the grade levels. You will be amazed by how effective this is in developing a positive feeling among the students for their principal and their school.

When you sit and eat with students (make sure to buy cafeteria food), you reveal human characteristics most students would not attribute to a principal. Some of the younger children have told us that they didn't know we really eat lunch like they do.

During this time, it is important for you to be a very good listener. Students are much more relaxed during lunch and are eager to share information with you. This information is helpful in planning for different areas of the school. Principals can always get a fresh view of activities that go on in the building by listening to the students and seeing the school from their perspective.

After having lunch with a class, walk around outside to see what they are doing during their free time. This time is valuable informal time, and often the more reluctant students will walk up to you and say hi. If you have the energy to kick a soccer ball or

- Food is an effective communication tool.
- Eat, but listen more.
- Record some notes back in your office after each meal.

throw a football during this time, you will be the topic of conversation at the dinner table in every household in your community.

THE LITTLE THINGS DO MATTER

As the chief administrator of a building, the principal spends a great deal of time involved in the global issues facing a school community. While this time is critical to the success of the school, remember not to lose sight of the little things that take place in a school each day.

The little things of school are just as important in setting the total tone and climate for the building. The little things are often not planned for and require a principal to be observant, efficient, and out of his or her office as often as possible.

The little things may include ensuring that the doors are locked after the students arrive, promptly returning calls to parents, ordering supplies on a timely basis, making sure all teachers arrived on time, preparing daily announcements, checking the halls for safety issues, stopping in the cafeteria to make sure the food for the day arrived, and remembering to see a specific child first thing in the morning.

- Stay in touch and in tune with the routine things in your building.
- Use visuals such as sticky notes to remind yourself of the little things to do.
- Attention to the small details often prevents major, negative issues from developing.

The list of little things to do can be endless, and many are easily forgotten about in the hectic schedule most principals must keep. Try keeping a running list of little things on sticky notes on your desk, which remind you to attend to those important little things as soon as possible.

BUY STOCK IN HALLMARK

Hand-in-hand with the little things is sending personal cards to staff members for particular occasions. This small task truly shows you care. Purchase a wide range of occasion cards during the summer and keep them in your desk for ready access.

Blank cards are especially effective. They allow you to write a specific message to an individual, which helps you to make a more personal connection than you could with store-purchased cards.

Sending a card, for even a small event, can have long-term positive results in building a spirit of team.

One principal regularly scans the comics in the newspaper for appropriate themes and topics. These can be used as part of a memo, to highlight a notepad, or to decorate a card. Many education journals also include cartoons that can be used in the same way.

> • Have a variety of cards available at all times in your desk.
> • Write specific, personal messages.

EVERYONE VALUES A BREAK

Time off during the course of a day is tough to find for any educator. When not directly involved with students, teachers and administrators are doing the necessary paperwork to do the job well. Why not give a teacher an unexpected half hour break? During the course of a year, make sure to take over every teachers' class at least once, for a half hour period of time. It is amazing how much that short break means to a teacher.

While the teacher is taking the unexpected and greatly appreciated time, spend the time talking to the students about their year in school and encourage them to share with you any issues they may have regarding the running of the school. Make a rule that they cannot discuss a particular teacher during this time, or your efforts will be wasted and you will create ill will.

The students enjoy the break that you gave their teacher, and during this time they often have great suggestions for improving the school community. Make sure that you take notes during the discussion. Then, try to implement the suggestions where appropriate and make sure that the students who offered the suggestions are aware of the change you made.

Most teachers will come back to their class well before the half hour is over and will sit in the back of the room, enjoying the exchange between you and their students. Word will spread quickly among staff members that you gave someone a break, and the teachers will jokingly ask when they will get their turn. Let their break time be a surprise—an unannounced break has a more lasting, positive effect.

> • A half hour break for a teacher is like a day off.
> • Use the half hour to gather only positive information and constructive suggestions from students.
> • Write the teacher a short note telling him or her how positive the class was.

LET THEM EAT ICE CREAM

Food is a universal icebreaker and creates good will no matter what the type of food or which time of year. Once or twice a year, host a morning breakfast for the entire staff. Open the breakfast to all members of the school community and do not keep an agenda other than your own, which is to create a bond among all of the school's constituents and to keep people in touch with each other.

An administrator we know recently told us that he had a Mister Softy ice cream truck come to the school during a staff development day. He interrupted the teachers in the middle of their lunchtime to announce that the ice cream truck was outside especially for them, and then he offered all staff members their choice of anything on the truck. The administrator said that he had never received as many thank-you notes from any other small gesture and that people are still talking about the ice cream truck. Small, unexpected nice things have a tremendous, positive effect on the atmosphere of a school building.

Other principals provide a coffee bar in the morning as a surprise or sponsor potluck staff lunches. One high school sponsors regular Friday lunches, for which each department provides dessert and the principal supplies coffee. This event, which started small, has led to a competitive spirit at the school: One department tries to outdo the next with fancy desserts and decorations. The idea worked, bringing a sense of unity to the school and moving staff members from their office or desk lunch to a community lunch.

- Giving a staff member a short break can have lasting value.
- Students value informal time with their principal.
- Ice cream makes everyone a child.

Chapter Seven

Self

The demands principals face today often create stress. From the emphasis on accountability, test scores, and rankings to legal issues, challenges, and problems, successfully navigating the complex world of schools is increasingly difficult. Principals often pay the price in the form of physical and emotional exhaustion.

Our final chapter offers a variety of activities and strategies to help principals attend to their own needs for professional growth and personal satisfaction. Whether it is keeping a journal, attending conferences, mentoring future leaders, or creating mini vacations during the workday and week, principals must devote thought, time, and energy to their own needs. We hope our suggestions prove useful to you, and we invite you to add to our list. Ultimately, you are the best judge of what meets your personal and professional needs.

KEEP A JOURNAL

Keeping a journal is a great way to reflect on issues and problems that face a principal. It can also become a very valuable historic record in addition to being an outlet for frustrations and dilemmas that principals wrestle with.

A journal itself can be anything as simple as a notebook of blank paper or as formal as a daybook with prompts and stimulating quotes. One principal uses a multiyear book that provides space for eleven years of writing, as well as numerous special pages in which to keep a record of different topics, such as doctor visits, car care, and so on. Journals often serve as a place to record new ideas. A small, easily carried notebook can serve this function well, allowing you to jot down ideas that pop up at the least expected time and places.

Journal writing is a very idiosyncratic practice, with some people writing extensively about themes, situations, people, or events and others writing only short, cryptic daily comments. There is no right way to keep a journal. All that matters is that the journal is convenient and comfortable for you. More principals are using laptop computers and electronic handheld devices, which allow principals to easily keep an electronic journal. Electronic journals allow you to print individual sections and to have the journal on hand anywhere you use a computer.

Many graduate courses make journaling a specific assignment. Recording how one perceives and deals with the myriad of situations that a school administrator faces can become an analytical tool as well as a means of reflection. One principal expanded her journal to include articles about her school and community. Another principal personalized his journal with copies of his annual yearbook page as well as inspirational quotes. Some principals find keeping a more practical journal that addresses specific school topics a valuable tool. One principal keeps a discipline journal that logs student issues and includes notes from investigations. Another principal keeps a phone log of all calls, with detailed notes and commentaries. These records provide valuable historical archives and an opportunity to identify and reflect on schoolwide changes and developments.

- Keep a reflective journal.
- Electronic journals are quick and efficient.
- Choose a journal format you are comfortable with.

The time invested in journaling is more often than not time well spent. Whether or not a principal finds the experience relaxing, he or she will always be able to make use of the journal as a factual record.

CONFERENCES

Attending conferences is often viewed as a perk or as a time commitment busy principals cannot fit into their schedules. However, attending conferences should be a regular item on each principal's yearly to-do list. Conferences provide positive opportunities to recharge one's batteries and to learn about programs and approaches that make principals more efficient and effective.

Many principals choose one of the major national yearly association conferences. Each major educational association offers a three- or four-day national conference that offers literally hundreds of sessions to choose from, three or four nationally known keynote speakers, and an impressive vendor display area.

The vendors alone are often worth the visit. Major book publishers, computer software companies, and educational retailers provide up-to-date information on products and offer a variety of giveaways. One principal was able to collect enough free pencils and pens to outfit the office for the year. Another principal selected a gift for each of the department chairs at his school from the many items collected.

While those attending conferences may be tempted to fill every waking second with a different session, the informal time and contacts made during a conference are just as valuable. Hearing about a new program or issues faced at schools in other parts of the country—and realizing that the challenges you face are the same throughout the country—helps put the job in perspective.

In addition to the national conferences, most associations sponsor regional conferences on specific topics or themes. If your school is dealing with a particular issue addressed by one of these conferences, you may want to attend along with some of the key opinion makers in your school community.

Occasionally, it is exciting to go outside the box and attend a conference that typically is not for educators. Many business-focused conferences address approaches to leadership, organizational design, and other business topics that have direct relation to the field of education. Networking with professionals in other fields also gives you a unique perspective when you return to your school.

While most conferences take place during the school year, there are special summer conferences and institutes that provide extended time to look at both a specific topic and school leadership in general. Many of the institutes build time in for reflective reading and writing as well as time for exercise and relaxation. Many colleges and universities host such summer conferences. Often the cost of a weeklong summer institute is less than a three- or four-day national conference because the institute is based on a college campus.

The end of a school year brings a special time for principal retreats. One county principals' association sponsors a three-day end-of-year retreat for high school and middle school principals. In addition to bringing in one or two state and national speakers, the retreat also provides principals sustained time to reflect and plan for the coming year.

Conferences also give a principal the chance to present on almost any topic. Writing a conference presentation proposal and giving the presentation require thoughtful preparation. In one sense, conference presentations turn the tables on a principal—the principal is the one being evaluated, and the presenter's colleagues write the evaluations.

Bringing teachers, students, or parents with you to a conference is another valuable use of the experience. Whether the group is going to study a particular topic, to present, or to simply experience the conference, going as a group can build the support and camaraderie so vital in building a positive school culture.

- Attending a conference is a great energizer.
- Visit vendors to get new ideas and replenish supplies.
- Network with other principals.
- Consider making a conference presentation.

Finally, for many principals, attending a conference is most important as a method to relax and escape the pressure and demands of school leadership. Your own mental and physical health is vital to being an effective principal.

STUDY GROUPS

Maintaining a broad perspective on schools and education is often a challenge for principals. One way to address this need is to join or form a study group or collegial circle.

The opportunity to think, reflect, and generate new ideas about issues and problems assists a principal in dealing with the daily demands of the job. A study group or collegial circle usually forms around a book, an article, or a topic. The composition of the group may range from a mixture of teachers and administrators in a single building or department to district- or areawide groups that bring individuals together from different districts and backgrounds. Often, professional development programs include options for creating and participating in study groups, with credit, salary, hours, or release time tied to the experience.

These groups meet at almost any time that is convenient for the members. One district sponsors collegial circles through its teacher center, holding after-school meetings. One county principals' association sponsors a group that meets over dinner once a month in an area restaurant. The retired teachers' group in our district meets over lunch in the high school and invites a current teacher each time to lead the discussion about a book.

As professional development expands both its scope and requirements, more staff members are choosing study groups. The dialogue and sharing give principals fresh ideas on how to approach and handle situations and issues. Hearing the problems and issues that face other schools and districts helps principals appreciate that issues in their own schools are actually not so bad.

An advantage of joining a group with other principals, especially if you are the only member from your district, is being able to share a problem that you need help with. Often, you can receive feedback and suggestions that would be hard to come by in your own district.

The study group experience also provides a model for organizing and running some of the committees that a principal must form. For example, committees charged with investigating a particular issue or problem are often expected to include a wide range of stakeholders with a variety of opinions. An approach that includes the study, review, and discussion of the literature on the subject provides an opportunity for all sides on the issue to be heard. A study group approach is far more effective in making sure all parties feel listened to than the traditional approach to committees.

> - Use a study group to address schoolwide issues.
> - Study groups serve as think tanks for schools.

PORTFOLIOS

Creating a portfolio of one's professional career and accomplishments can be a rewarding exercise and provide the material needed to apply for a job or a special award. A portfolio also serves as an historical record that contains material about your school and yourself. This is a great project for the summer and should be a regular part of the yearly culling and organizing of files and materials.

A few simple supplies are needed to create a useful and easily updateable portfolio. A large, three-ring binder, a pack of plastic protector sheets, and a number of tabbed dividers are all you need to be on your way. Divide the binder into sections and include sections for your resume, letters of commendation and awards, key projects, a list of references, news articles about you or your school, memos that address important examples of your leadership, sample staff evaluations you wrote, certifications, college transcripts, and diplomas.

Technology offers the opportunity to include pictures, videos, audiotapes, and even a CD-ROM with a collection of your work.

The portfolio is a great tool to take on job interviews. You can easily remove a section to circulate among the interviewers on a specific topic, or you can share the entire notebook if needed.

> - Create a professional portfolio.
> - Technology allows for pictures, videos, and audio material.
> - Portfolios are great preparation for a job search.

PREPARING FUTURE PRINCIPALS

Helping prepare future principals is a way to stay energized and focused on your job. As a mentor, you may be giving potential leaders opportunities to experience the demands and excitement of the role by allowing them to be principal for a day, or you may be telling your war stories in the faculty room. Either way, you are helping to develop the educational leaders of tomorrow, a very real need as so many current principals near retirement.

Leadership develops from commitment, talent, and experience. As a sitting principal, mentoring staff members who have expressed interest in becoming a principal and encouraging bright young teachers to consider an administrative career are ways for you to reflect on the challenges and issues facing principals. Many local principals' associations have made the recruiting and training of the next generation of school leaders a priority. For example, one county association in New York sponsors an annual series of leadership seminars to which current principals can bring aspiring administrators as guests. The seminars are taught by members of the association and address issues that range from hiring teachers to handling difficult parents or staff. Teaching one of these seminars is a great way for principals to reflect on issues and share skills and experiences that otherwise might go unshared (see Resource E for a sample seminar overview).

Creating leadership opportunities and experiences within your school for interested faculty is a way to address building needs and to assist in the development of the next group of school leaders. Whether it is asking someone to chair a committee or creating structures that empower faculty, you can help solve the dilemma of how to get it all done by sharing responsibility and power.

Many area colleges and universities have become willing partners by basing administrative certification programs in area public schools. Hosting courses at your school produces a cadre of faculty members who are looking for leadership experiences but who might not have the resources to attend a university. While attending courses, your faculty can accept specific projects or tasks—and perhaps even some problems—to meet course requirements.

> - Mentor future principals.
> - Create leadership opportunities for your aspiring administrators.
> - Share your experiences and knowledge.

Reflection, careful analysis, and the sharing of stories all help prepare future leaders and, at the same time, help focus and energize principals to continue their work. On a practical level, empowering others gives you assistance with day-to-day tasks and makes more time for you to lead.

ADMINISTRATIVE RETREATS

The routines and patterns of life in school make finding time for thoughtful and sustained discussion difficult. Often, administrative cabinet meetings become forums to resolve immediate problems or to vent frustrations that build as administrators respond to the pressures of the moment. More often than not, members are called away or do not even make meetings because they are pressed to attend to an immediate crisis. Rarely are significant educational questions and issues addressed in such rushed and hectic settings.

For a relatively small cost in time and dollars, principals can lead retreats for their key staff. By taking a group to an off-school site—for a morning, day, or overnight—principals have the opportunity to forge interpersonal bonds and create the time and atmosphere needed to carefully study questions and issues that require sustained time to process and resolve.

The site for a retreat can range from a familiar local restaurant or hotel to an eclectic art gallery or outdoor education facility. One principal brought her team to her vacation home and in a few hours accomplished what would have taken weeks of meetings. Another principal rented a room at the county art museum and combined intense discussions of student assessment practices with a tour of the gallery. Some principals connect with local businesses or universities and use their facilities. The cost for this may well end up coming in the form of a donation (see Resource F for a sample retreat memo to staff).

Planning the retreat is a wonderful opportunity to engage staff in considering the big picture. A retreat also offers the principal the challenge and the opportunity to select teachers to act as the administrator in charge while the retreat participants are off site.

The investment of time in planning, carrying out, and implementing the results of a retreat experience is worth the effort. The experience is often energizing to both the individuals who attend and to the other constituents of the school. Whether the retreat is a summer activity or a day off during the school year, engaging the staff in planning the retreat is a must. One good source of topics can be those issues that go unresolved at the regular administrative meetings. Keep a list of these issues and questions and refer back to them in planning the theme and structure of the retreat.

- Plan a yearly retreat for your administrative staff.
- Address big-picture issues at the retreat.
- Retreats energize a school.

PAMPER YOURSELF

Much of this book focused on efficient ways to successfully manage the extraordinary number of tasks and responsibilities principals face each day. By adopting and adapting some of the suggestions we shared in this book, a principal can find time to take an instructional leadership role that will make a positive difference.

In addition to these strategies, principals need to create ways to reward themselves and to replenish their energy. In short, principals need mini vacations—a few minutes or a few hours, depending on the need and the circumstance.

Find opportunities for a few minutes of relaxation. For example, after four nights of meetings and events, sleep in one day and come in late. Make time to eat a leisurely breakfast, read the paper, and complete the crossword puzzle. In the midst of another long day, close the door, put your feet up, and close your eyes for fifteen minutes. Keep a blanket or exercise mat in the office for just such a time. Having music available to sooth your mood also works to recharge one's batteries. Take a walk, not just around the halls but use also the grounds, especially on those beautiful fall or spring days. Leave the building for a few minutes to get a cup of coffee or to take a ride to pick up your clothes from the cleaners, or do as many principals do and go watch the students learning or performing because that is ultimately what the job is all about.

Given the stress of the job and the time demands of the role, principals need to find an approach that keeps them rested and fit. Whether it is an afternoon nap or a brisk walk, an hour in the weight room or a healthy salad for dinner rather than a heavy meal, principals must be attentive to the rhythms of their bodies and the need to focus clearly on each person or issue that comes their way. Attending to one's own needs is as important as returning all those phone calls.

- Maintain your energy and optimism by taking mini vacations.
- Exercise, exercise, exercise.
- Attend to your own needs.

TEACH A CLASS

Instructional leadership is all about teaching and learning. Many principals lose touch with the realities of the classroom given the demands on their time and the ever-changing nature of school programs and practices. It is vitally important for principals to do more than observe a few classes each year. Making time to teach is a priority every principal should embrace.

Making time to teach requires creativity and careful planning. Whether it is teaching a lesson to cover a teacher's class or teaching a yearlong course, principals can and should make the time to refresh their classroom skills and connect with their students. Even more important, the preparation to teach and the act itself is a renewing activity that often restores faith and idealism about students.

The practical steps to teach include forging an agreement with the teachers' union, finding a time of day that fits your schedule and temperament, and selecting subject matter that you have expertise in and are comfortable with. Approaches include designing a short (few days or a week) unit on a topic and teaching only that unit or teaching a complete course. One school anticipated the value of their principal teaching and designed a building that included a classroom adjacent to the principal's office. The space also doubles as a conference room.

Teaching offers a principal the chance to invite colleagues in to observe and critique the teaching. This helps establish a practice that encourages teachers to observe and assist each other. It also makes a statement about the priorities of the school's leader.

Some principals enjoy covering a teacher's class to allow the teacher to attend a meeting or professional development activity. This often creates a situation that permits the principal to seek feedback from the students about the school and hear any concerns that students may have. It also provides an opportunity for the students and principal to brainstorm ideas to make the school a better place.

Some cautions should be kept in mind when taking on the role of teacher. Principals should make every effort to cover classes across departments or grade levels. When teaching a course, be sure to structure it so that you are not perceived as taking a section away from a teacher. This can easily become a union issue if you have not made an agreement in advance. It also goes without saying that the principal's class preparation and delivery should be of the highest quality. In short, do not take this role unless you are willing and able to handle the attention and scrutiny you will face.

- Make time to teach.
- Connect with students through teaching.
- Work with your teachers' associations to make your teaching a positive experience for all.

READING AND SHARING

Given the time demands on a principal, reading seems to be a luxury that one can ill afford. To the contrary, reading is a critical part of being an effective school leader. Whether by reading articles that highlight the accomplishments of your students, alumni, or staff or that detail the inevitable tragedies that befall communities, principals have the responsibility of reading the news to ensure that all appropriate parties are made aware of current events. In addition, numerous professional articles and books need to be reviewed and shared with staff. So how does a principal do it all?

Subscribe to local newspapers and a variety of educational and leadership journals. Clip and copy articles that staff will find interesting and valuable. Many articles can be found on the Internet and can be e-mailed or printed for sharing. One principal sends copies of articles about his students home with them, along with a note of commendation.

Make sure your budget includes funds to purchase educational books. Pass them along to interested staff, along with a copy of reviews or articles related to the book or topic. One effective vehicle for promoting staff dialogue is to form a collegial circle to read and discuss a particular book. One area school has a retired teacher group that is led by a current teacher, and the group discusses a new book in each meeting.

Often, principals rely on educational journals and books for their main sources of information. Break out of this habit and subscribe to journals for business, technology, and the arts. Principals can frequently find ideas and articles that relate in a different way to school issues.

Aspiring principals often choose the field because they have worked either for a very successful and popular principal or because they toil in a school with weak and ineffective leadership. Principals who recognize the reasons for their choice consciously model behaviors and practices designed to encourage others to take on the challenge of leading a school. One principal uses the faculty welcome-back letter each year to share one or more of the books read over the summer that relate to educational issues facing the school. Another principal offers faculty and parents the opportunity to provide a written evaluation of the year and to make suggestions for the principal to improve his or her work.

> - Read, read, and read some more.
> - Share articles, books, and news clippings with staff.
> - Expand your reading to areas outside of education topics.

Resource A

Today's Agenda

Done   *Things That Must Be Done Today*

_____   1. _____
_____   2. _____
_____   3. _____
_____   4. _____
_____   5. _____
_____   6. _____
_____   7. _____
_____   8. _____
_____   9. _____
_____   10. _____
_____   11. _____
_____   12. _____
_____   13. _____
_____   14. _____
_____   15. _____

Telephone Calls

_____   _____   Re: _____
_____   _____   Re: _____
_____   _____   Re: _____
_____   _____   Re: _____
_____   _____   Re: _____
_____   _____   Re: _____
_____   _____   Re: _____
_____   _____   Re: _____
_____   _____   Re: _____
_____   _____   Re: _____

Correspondence and Projects

_____   _____
_____   _____
_____   _____
_____   _____
_____   _____
_____   _____
_____   _____

Resource B

Yearly Task List

JULY

Revise teacher handbook

Department chair summer meeting dates with new teacher orientation information

Summer letter to staff

Revise administrative responsibilities

Plan ninth-grade orientation

Set up meeting dates for faculty, administration, counselors, central administration

Maintenance tour of building

Letter to ninth graders and new students regarding orientation

Fill cocurricular positions

Letter to new teachers with copies to department chairs

Revise student calendar and handbook

Plan music trip

Create list of what goes into August mailings for families

AUGUST

Develop goals, projects, objectives

Letter to parents and students for opening of school

Letter to students regarding parking

Plan new teacher orientation

Meeting with HSA president to set dates, goals, coffee dates, etc.

Set up plans and dates for guidance evenings

Opening day for staff plans

Supervisory assignments completed

Department chair guidelines and meeting dates with professional development

Assignments

Set field trip cutoff date

Mail student schedules

Plan freshman parent/student evening

Set fire drill schedule for year

SEPTEMBER

Committee opportunities memo with initial meeting dates

Sunshine committee meeting

Meeting with switchboard regarding PA announcements during school

Wellness/Drug-free plans

Dawn Patrol memo

Football call chart

Fund-raisers memo

Posting signs memo

Program monitoring reports from department chairs due

Back to School Night prep

Back to School Night letter

Coop letter with expectations

Review bomb threat policy

Credit letters

Assistant principals—review search, campus police procedures

Set up schedule of observations and performance reviews with assistant principals

Select department chairs for yeark

Schedule four required faculty meetings:
affirmative action in newsletter

Department staff development plans

Record keeping for twelve hours of meeting time for faculty

Set up schedule of CHEA liaison meetings

Opening student assemblies—security, theft problem

NHS selection process

Set up guidance newsletter schedule

Set objectives with assistant principals

Meeting with cocurricular advisors regarding
supervision, eligibility

Meetings with new teachers

Set up student leaders meetings

Emergency calling lists

Memo to faculty regarding ADD student program

OCTOBER

Program monitoring reports from department
chairs to central office

Schedule of meetings with East principal

Back to School Night—thanks to ROTC, SGO, maintenance, staff

Curriculum proposals

Budget development for next school year

Fall pep rally plans

Yearbook letter

Complete all state reports

NOVEMBER

Congrats letter to honor roll students with bumper stickers

DECEMBER

Holiday parties memo

Supplemental and capital budget lists

IDEA application

Gifts for office staff

JANUARY

Interim meetings with department chairs

Eighth-grade parent meeting preparation

Course selection

Assistant principal assessments

Hold elective fair

FEBRUARY

Department chair nontenured annual performance reviews

Congratulation letter to Hall of Fame

Write president for graduation letter of congratulations

Letter of welcome—Jazz Festival

Secretary and aide evaluations

Congrats letter to second marking period honor roll

MARCH

Staffing projections

Plans for PAVAS

Closing procedures

APRIL

Scheduling

Graduation preparation

Congrats letter to third marking period honor roll

MAY

Letter to seniors regarding senior meeting

Department chair/student activities coordinator annual performance reviews

Assistant principals final assessment

Department chair party

Reports on committee work for year

Send failure warning letters

Teacher appreciation day

Twenty-five year mark for teachers' list

"Lion" in awards

Final exam schedule

In-class final exam memo

Cheating on finals memo

HAS department award winners

Cocurricular recommendations for next year and memo with openings

Closing procedures

Administrators' vacation

Senior exit interviews

Complete extracurricular enrollment report

JUNE

Project graduation ticket sales, faculty and chaperone memo

Summer work recommendations

Department chair summer meeting dates and work schedule

Faculty summer interviews schedule

School calendar sheet

Resource C

Faculty Note Cards

Ellen Holzman   Eng

7 th as teacher
Wheatley grad
9 th as parent
Putts connection "The Voice" editor
9 th   / SWS / Proj Adv
(2)   (1)   2 sections

Rudderless — need for leadership
+ for Humanities
10 th issue as 1 st split SWS/ IOP/ SO
(often (8 th, 9 th not a prob)
Yearbook
Perf Review : writing own poetry

Randy Stander   Bus Ed

5 th on coming up
Perf Eval : reassess dept course offerings
              update "MAC" software
B— Ball card collector
daughter frosh Binghamton
looking at work — study curv

Resource D

Student
Planner Memo

MEMORANDUM

TO: All Faculty
FROM: Richard A. Simon
DATE: September 4, 2003
RE: SCHOOL AGENDA BOOKS

All students and faculty will be receiving 2003–2004 school agenda books this week. The agenda books are designed to assist students in keeping organized as well as provide a number of useful tools to improve academic performance. The agenda books also contain important Wheatley information previously distributed as individual handouts. Specifically, the agenda book includes the district calendar (pp. 2–3), the guidelines for behavior (pp. 5–16), the guidance program (pp. 17–20), the Interscholastic guidelines (pp. 21–27), and a comprehensive description of clubs and activities (pp. 28–48).

Student agenda books will be distributed in English classes on Tuesday and Wednesday, September 4th and 5th. Teacher editions are in your opening-of-school packets. A limited number of covers are available for purchase through the school store for $7.00. Replacement agenda books may be purchased in the main office for $5.00 each.

The publisher has provided us with extensive materials to support and enhance the use of the agenda books. I have attached a few sample materials, which you may want to make use of. The complete notebook of materials may be borrowed from my office. I also have a number of laminated wall charts designed to use when making assignments. Please feel free to pick one up from my office.

I strongly encourage you to model the use of the agenda book and expect each of your students to use it regularly. If we all reinforce this expectation, the agenda book will quickly become a valuable tool for every student. I look forward to your suggestions in making the book a valuable part of our school program.

Resource E

Aspiring Administrator Training Brochure

**HOFSTRA UNIVERSITY SCHOOL
LEADERSHIP SEMINAR SERIES**

Purpose

To provide a forum for high school principals, aspiring administrators, and college professors to:

- Meet and discuss issues of school leadership
- Encourage potential administrators to consider the high school principalship as a career goal
- Explore the emerging challenges of the principalship

Sponsors

- Nassau County High School Principals Association
- Hofstra University Center for Secondary School Administrators and Supervisors
- Nassau County School Leadership Center
- Long Island School Leadership Center

Format

- Three late afternoon sessions (4–7 P.M.) including a light dinner held at Hofstra University, Scott Skodnek Business Development Center, Room 210
- Nassau County high school principals will lead all sessions

Dates and Topics

- Wednesday, January 8, 2003: "Sharing Substance Abuse Prevention Programs"
  Presenters: Bernard Kaplan and Carol Burris

- Wednesday, February 12, 2003: "Creating an Effective Marketing/Public Relations Program"
  Presenters: Yvette Villagas and Arthur Jonas

- Wednesday, March 5, 2003: "Effective Time Management for High School Leaders"
  Presenters: Randy Ross and Joyce Bisso

Participants

- Nassau County high school principals
- At least one aspiring administrator invited by each participating principal. *Note:* This year each participating principal may invite up to three aspiring administrators
- Hofstra University faculty

Be Part of This Special Program—Register Now

(Fees and registration information attached)

SOURCE: Reprinted with permission of Hofstra University.

Resource F

Administrative Retreat Memo

MEMORANDUM

DATE: December 9, 2002
TO: Academic Board
FROM: Rick
RE: Retreat

I hope you are looking forward to our academic board retreat this Friday, December 13, 2002. We will meet at the Nassau County Art Museum at 10:00 A.M. in the library of the main museum building. To reach the museum, take Glen Cove Road north to Northern Boulevard and then head west on Northern Boulevard. The museum grounds are on your right, about 1/10 of a mile before you reach the Roslyn viaduct.

The program for the day is as follows:

10:00 to 11:00 A.M.: Meeting/discussion time
11:00 A.M. to 2:00 P.M.: Tour of the museum collection
12:00 P.M. to 3:00 P.M.: Meeting/discussion time, including lunch

Based on some of our meetings this year, the following topics may warrant further attention:

1. The exam weighting system

2. The process and standards used to determine access to honors and advanced placement classes

3. The implementation of the new attendance policy and the role of the attendance coordinator

4. The implementation of the Grade 8 Committee recommendations and the role of the eighth-grade coordinator

5. The academic standard (G.P.A.) for admission to the National Honor Society

6. The objectives to considered as part of the AFG process

We will also devote a good deal of time to discussing your reactions to Denise Pope's book *Doing School.* You will find a copy of the discussion questions for the book on the back of this memo.

I look forward to a day of good company, thoughtful and provoking discussion, and art.

DISCUSSION QUESTIONS

"Doing School": How We Are Creating a Generation of Stressed Out, Materialistic, and Miseducated Students

By Denise Clark Pope

1. How do Wheatley students "do school"? What compromises do our students make to succeed here?

2. Do many of our students see the focus of school as "getting good grades, rather than on actually learning the material?"

3. What "treaties" have teachers established with students at Wheatley? What "treaties" have we established between teachers and the administration?

4. How can we create an environment that encourages the formation of mentor-type relationships between more students, all students, and teachers?

5. Does Wheatley "promote deception, hostility, and anxiety" as the author speculates Faircrest does?

6. Does the Wheatley system support intellectual engagement and passion?

7. What could we do at Wheatley to "humanize" the high school experience more?

8. What could we do to the curriculum to improve the educational experience for all students?

9. How can we do a better job of working closely with our students? How can we listen to our students' needs, frustrations, and desires?

**CORWIN
PRESS**

The Corwin Press logo—a raven striding across an open book—represents the happy union of courage and learning. We are a professional-level publisher of books and journals for K-12 educators, and we are committed to creating and providing resources that embody these qualities. Corwin's motto is "Success for All Learners."